Withdrawn

Data Wise

Data Wise

**A Step-by-Step Guide
to Using Assessment Results
to Improve Teaching
and Learning**

EDITED BY

KATHRYN PARKER BOUDETT

ELIZABETH A. CITY

RICHARD J. MURNANE

Harvard Education Press
Cambridge, Massachusetts

Third Printing, 2006

Library of Congress Control Number 2005931449

Paperback ISBN 1-891792-67-9
Library Edition ISBN 1-891792-68-7

Published by Harvard Education Press,
an imprint of the Harvard Education Publishing Group

Harvard Education Press
8 Story Street
Cambridge, Massachusetts 02138

Cover and interior design: Anne Carter

The typefaces used in this book are ITC new Baskerville and Gill Sans.

TABLE OF CONTENTS

PREFACE

IN AN EFFORT TO DETERMINE how best to prepare school leaders to use student assessment results to improve teaching and learning, a group consisting of faculty and doctoral students at the Harvard Graduate School of Education (HGSE) and school leaders from three Boston public schools worked together for two years. This book is a product of our collective knowledge about what school leaders need to know and do to ensure that the piles of student assessment results landing on their desks are used to improve student learning in their schools.

The contributors to this book are a varied group with quite different experiences and expertise. Three of us are urban public school principals; one of us directs out-of-school programs in an urban public school; several of us are HGSE faculty members, one a statistician, one an economist, one a scholar of assessment issues, and one a public policy analyst. Some of us are HGSE doctoral students, with experience in urban, suburban, and independent schools across the country. All of us have worked in or with urban schools, where we have struggled with the issues that we write about in this book. Most of us have extensive teaching experience; some of us also have worked as guidance counselors, coaches, or administrators. What we share is a commitment to provide all children with a good education, and a belief that thoughtful, systematic, collaborative examination of student assessment results can contribute to this goal.

Forging new knowledge was the core activity that led us to create this book. We met regularly for more than two hours at a time during the school year, engaging frequently in intense conversations about difficult issues. For example, some of our members who had extensive experience as classroom teachers felt it made no sense to spend a lot of time examining results from high-stakes tests. Other members, especially school principals, felt such work was a valuable starting place. Adherents of both positions argued effectively and helped the group appreciate the importance of examining a wide range of data sources.

Another example concerns preparation for tests. Some group members felt it was critical to devote instructional time to preparing students to take high-stakes exams. Others argued that test preparation artificially inflated scores so that the scores did not reflect transferable knowledge. Forging a common understanding between principals who were under intense pressure to improve test scores and assessment experts who were wary of score inflation was a challenge. However, our common commitment to improve the quality of education for urban children led us to seek common ground. The thoughtful suggestions each of us made about the many drafts of every chapter helped us to find it. We frequently came back to the question of whether the content and tone of each chapter would make it useful to school leaders who were focused on improving instruction and increasing student learning.

While we have urban roots, we see our approach to using data and our examples for illuminating it as relevant to educators working in all kinds of schools. We designed the two composite case studies we featured in the book to reflect many of the challenges educators in schools across the country face today.

Many people and organizations contributed to making this book possible. Rather than simply listing them, we provide a brief description of the activities that led to the creation of our seminar group and the people who made it possible.

In spring 2001, Harvard professor Richard Murnane arranged with Boston Public Schools (BPS) superintendent Thomas Payzant to spend the next school year helping the BPS central office improve the support it offered schools in how to learn from student assessment results. One of the first things Murnane learned in planning the year was that several groups were already actively engaged in helping Boston's public schools learn from student assessment results. Of particular importance were the BPS central office staff and the Boston Plan for Excellence (BPE), BPS's external partner.

At BPS, Maryellen Donahue, director of the Office of Research, Assessment, and Evaluation, Al Lau, director of the Office of Information Systems, and Ann Grady, director of the Office of Information Technology, had jointly created a software tool called LIZA (the acronym for Local Intranet Zone for Administrators), which allowed BPS principals to obtain information electronically on the students in their schools. One of LIZA's strengths was that it provided access to student data from the BPS central student database, which was updated every night. This was important, because with a mobile student population, the students enrolled in certain schools in January were quite a different group from the students enrolled there the previous September. One significant limitation of LIZA was that it was not created to support the analysis of patterns in student assessment results, and therefore was difficult to use for that purpose. So while a few computer-savvy principals did use LIZA to download data that they then analyzed in a spreadsheet program, most did not. A second limitation was that teachers did not have access to LIZA.

In response to requests from BPS principals for help in analyzing student assessment results, Ellen Guiney, executive director of the Boston Plan for Excellence, asked Kristan Singleton, then the BPE technology director, to create desktop software dedicated to this purpose. Singleton led a group that created FAST Track, a software with the virtue of being easy to use. By 2001, more than 40 Boston public schools were using the new software to create school-level portraits of student achievement. However, FAST Track also had its limitations. Most importantly, it used student data that the school principals could request from the BPS central office and that a BPE staffer loaded onto each school's desktop computer at the beginning of the school year. Schools with mobile student populations had to repeat this time-consuming process frequently over the school year. A second limitation was that FAST Track updates had to be loaded onto each school's computer by BPE staff, another time-consuming process.

In the process of working with Boston's public schools on data use, the BPS and BPE staffs were learning a lot. So were HGSE doctoral students who were working with selected Boston public schools on data use under the auspices of the Harvard Office of School Partnerships. Yet the groups worked separately and did not learn from each other or pool their knowledge to figure out how to support schools more effectively.

To facilitate such learning, Maryellen Donahue and Richard Murnane invited individuals working on data issues with BPS to participate in a workshop dedicated to learning how to make the work more effective. Approximately 20 people accepted the invitation, and the workshop met for two hours every other week over the school year. Out of the workshop came the realization that BPS needed a data-and-software system that would allow BPS principals and teachers to efficiently examine test scores for their students.

Near the end of the 2001–02 school year, the Boston Plan for Excellence and the Boston Public Schools agreed to pool the knowledge they acquired in developing LIZA and FAST Track and to work together to create such a data system. Moreover, they decided to make the software a part of MyBPS, a comprehensive Web-based system, designed by a team headed by Albert Lau and Alice Santiago, that provided Boston's schools with a wide range of information. The result was MyBPS Assessment, a system that combined the strengths of LIZA and FAST Track and is now used by all Boston schools to analyze student assessment results. Several contributors to this volume worked on this project and learned many of the lessons described in this book.

Once the MyBPS Assessment software became available, the next challenge was to provide support so BPS educators could learn to use it. Again, the Harvard Graduate School of Education, the Boston Public Schools, and the Boston Plan for Excellence worked together to respond to this need. Together they staffed and funded the creation of a year-long course that taught teams of educators from BPS and HGSE students how to make constructive use of student assessment results.

In 2003, Kathryn Boudett became the lead instructor in the data course, with support from HGSE doctoral students Elizabeth City and Liane Moody. Boudett had led a research project for BPE designed to illuminate best practices in data use in Boston. Moody had contributed to this work and had played a key role in developing the MyBPS Assessment software as a member of the BPE staff. City had served as a literacy coach and change coach for BPS and was acutely aware of the challenges urban school faculties faced in learning to make constructive use of student assessment results. Over the next two years the teaching team developed new strategies for teaching critical skills to teams from 17 Boston public schools. Many of the ideas described in this book were developed in the process of planning and teaching this course, including the design of the improvement cycle around which this book is organized.

Before we began concrete work on this book, Thomas Payzant, Maryellen Donahue, Albert Lau, and Ann Grady of the Boston Public Schools had created an environment that made the book project possible. The Boston Plan for Excellence, under the leadership of executive director Ellen Guiney, supported the creation of the MyBPS Assessment, the training of BPS educators, and the development of the data course. Kristan Singleton, BPE assistant director, played a critical role in orchestrating BPE's vital contribution to the development of the MyBPS Assessment. Ellen Lagemann, dean of HGSE from 2002 to 2005, helped make the data course and the book seminar possible.

Once we began research and writing, many other individuals made valuable contributions to our work. We extend our sincerest thanks to the many educators who read all or parts of the draft manuscript and provided comments that helped us strengthen the book: Adrienne Chisolm, Hunter Credle, Stefanie Reinhorn, Oscar Santos, and Sara Schwartz Chrismer. These individuals helped us ground our case study schools' approach to improving instruction in sound and realistic practices. We also thank Tim Dugan of Kestrel Heights School in Durham, North Carolina, and Rob Matheson of Apex High School in Apex, North Carolina, for helping us understand their state's student assessment system.

A number of our Harvard colleagues also helped to frame our work. HGSE professor Richard Elmore helped us define and understand the idea of a problem of practice, an important term in chapter 5. HGSE professor Katherine Boles pushed us to think carefully about what it means to write for an audience of school leaders. HGSE professor Robert Schwartz introduced us and our ideas to Director Douglas Clayton and assistant director Caroline Chauncey of the Harvard Education Publishing Group. They embraced our ideas for a book and helped us turn it into a reality.

Caroline Chauncey's contributions went beyond providing good ideas for developing the arguments and sharpening the prose. During the 2004-05 school year, she came to our monthly workshop meetings and answered our many questions about how to turn our chapters into a coherent, useful book. Chris City did a marvelous job of editing and improving the manuscript; we are grateful for his dedication to the project during the most intense phase of the writing. Wendy Angus gave critical logistical support for the book seminar and for the book production.

The work that resulted in this book would not have been possible without financial support. Under the guidance of Marshall Smith, a longtime advocate of using data to guide instructional improvement, The William and Flora Hewlett Foundation was an early supporter of both BPE's FAST Track initiative and Murnane's work in Boston. Subsequent critical support for the research that led to this book was provided by The Spencer Foundation and by William and Juliana Thompson. We thank these individuals and organizations for their faith in the value of our unconventional project.

Some of the most important contributors to the ideas described in this book are the many BPS educators and HGSE graduate students who participated in the HGSE-BPS data course and allowed us to learn about the challenges in using assessment results to improve teaching and learning. As an indication of our appreciation for their support, all of the royalties from this book will be donated to the Harvard Graduate School of Education for work with the Boston Public Schools.

INTRODUCTION

Kathryn Parker Boudett, Elizabeth A. City, and Richard J. Murnane

THE PACKAGE CONTAINING DATA FROM LAST SPRING'S mandatory state exam landed with a thud on principal Roger Bolton's desk. The local newspaper had already published an article listing Franklin High (for the second year) as a school "in need of improvement" for failing to increase the percentage of tenth graders scoring well enough on the English language arts and mathematics exams to receive high school diplomas. Now this package from the state offered the gory details. Roger had five years of packages like this one, sharing shelf space with binders and boxes filled with results from the other assessments required by the district and state. The sheer mass of paper was overwhelming.

Frustrated as a teacher by how little Franklin expected of its students academically, Roger had vowed that when he became principal he would make it his mission to "get the learning up." But now, this heavy package reminded him that he would be judged primarily by whether he could "get the test scores up." He wanted to believe that there was something his faculty could learn from all these numbers that would help them increase student learning and get the scores up. But he didn't know where to start.

Many school leaders across the nation share Roger's frustration—a lack of knowledge about how to transform mountains of data on student achievement into an action plan that will improve instruction and increase student learning. Others have made some progress in responding to this challenge, but have become stymied along the way. Some have learned to identify patterns in student assessment results, but have not figured out what to do next. Some have not been able to convince their colleagues of the value of this work. Some have developed action plans, but have not been able to implement them. Some have implemented plans for improving instruction, but do not know how to evaluate their effectiveness. The goal of this book is to help educators in all of these positions to learn how to analyze data in a manner that contributes to improved instruction and increased student learning.

When we use the term "data," we mean not only scores on high-stakes tests, but also the broad array of other information on student skills and knowledge typically available in schools. For example, a growing number of districts administer "benchmark assessments" to gauge students' readiness for high-stakes exams. Some districts also administer end-of-course exams. Some schools assess student achievement with science fairs or exhibitions at which student projects are graded using agreed-upon rubrics. Then, of course, there are the classroom tests, projects, and homework that individual teachers assign to students as they work their way through the curriculum. These are just some of the kinds of data that educators can fruitfully examine in targeting areas for instructional improvement.

When we use the term "school leaders," we mean not only principals, but also the teacher leaders, directors of instruction, department heads, and coaches who are committed to engaging their colleagues in improving instruction at their school. A central premise underlying this book is that a good school is not a collection of good teachers working independently, but a team of skilled educators working together to implement a coherent instructional plan, to identify the learning needs of every student, and to meet those needs. We believe that the process of learning from data contributes to building an effective school and to helping the school continue to improve its performance.

A NEW CHALLENGE

The long-term evidence from the National Assessment of Educational Progress (NAEP) shows that average reading and math scores of today's 9-, 13-, and 17-year-olds are a little higher than they were in the 1970s. This is consistent with the view of most educators that they are working as hard as they can and are accomplishing at least as much as their colleagues did 30 years ago. So why the enormous external pressure to improve schools, as embodied in state accountability systems and the annual yearly progress (AYP) requirements of the federal No Child Left Behind (NCLB) legislation?

To a large extent, the answer lies in changes in the economy that have dramatically reduced earnings opportunities for Americans who leave school without strong reading, writing, and math skills and the knowledge of how to use these skills to acquire new knowledge and solve new problems. These striking long-term changes in the American economy provide much of the motivation for the standards movement and for the pressure American schools face to improve student learning.

A complementary source of pressure is the persistent and sizable gap between the average academic skills of white students and those of students of color. Unless this gap is closed, workers of color will increasingly be denied access to the growing number of jobs that require problem-solving and communication skills and that pay enough to support a family. This achievement gap helps to explain why pressure to improve education is particularly great in urban schools that serve high percentages of students of color.

Although the economic changes that provided the impetus for the standards movement were not created by the nation's educators, educators are under great pressure to respond to them by dramatically improving the quality of instruction children receive in school. We believe that the ideas in this book will help educators improve instruction and increase student learning. Moreover, we see this as a worthy goal not only because it will help the next generation of Americans earn enough to support their children, but also because it will give them the skills to contribute to civic life in a democracy beset by a host of problems.

What effective schools look like is not a mystery. They have a coherent instructional program well-aligned with strong standards. They have a community of adults committed to working together to develop the skills and knowledge of all children. They have figured out how to find the time to do this work and are acquiring the skills to do it well. This book is written for those educators who are committed to this work. We maintain that analyzing a variety of student assessment results can contribute to fulfilling their goals, if careful attention is paid to the limitations of tests and the technical challenges in interpreting student responses.

When students receive consistent high-quality instruction, scores on high-stakes tests rise. However, the converse need not be true. Faced with pressure to improve test scores, some educators analyze student assessment results to identify students who need just a few more points to pass a graduation exam, with the intent of improving these students' test-taking skills. Preparing students to pass the exams required for high school graduation is clearly important. However, it is more important that the time be spent helping students develop the skills they will need after graduation.

Some educators examine tests to identify frequently used questions and item formats so they can devote instructional time to helping students do well on particular tests. Familiarizing students with the format of high-stakes tests makes sense. So does explaining strategies to improve scores, such as answering every open-ended response question. However, the line between ensuring that students are test savvy and focusing scarce instructional time on preparing for a particular high-stakes test is a thin one. While "drill and kill" may lead to improved scores, it will not prepare students to thrive in our increasingly complex society.

STRUCTURING IMPROVEMENT: A ROAD MAP

For school leaders like principal Roger Bolton, the barriers to constructive, regular use of student assessment data to improve instruction can seem insurmountable. There is just so much data. Where do you start? How do you make time for the work? How do you build your faculty's skill in interpreting data sensibly? How do you build a culture that focuses on improvement, not blame? How do you maintain momentum in the face of all the other demands at your school? This book addresses all of these questions, providing strategies and tools for identifying possible explanations for strong and weak student performance, for examining the importance of alternative explanations, and for planning and executing instructional strategies to improve teaching and learning.

We have found that organizing the work of instructional improvement around a process that has specific, manageable steps helps educators build confidence and skill in using data. This process includes eight distinct activities school leaders can do to use their student assessment data effectively. Each activity is the focus of one chapter. We see the eight activities as falling into three categories: Prepare, Inquire, and Act.

We use the Data Wise Improvement Process graphic shown on the next page to illustrate the cyclical nature of the work. Initially, schools engage in a set of activities (i.e., prepare) to establish a foundation for learning from student assessment results. They then inquire, and subsequently act on what they learned. They then cycle back to further inquiry.

Prepare is about putting in place the structure for data analysis and looking at existing data from standardized tests. Chapter 1 describes tasks involved in organizing for collaborative work, including setting up a data team and taking stock of existing data. Chapter 2 explains key elements of assessment literacy that are critical to interpreting test results correctly.

Inquire is about acquiring the knowledge necessary to decide how to increase student learning. Chapter 3 describes the tasks involved in creating a data overview, especially how to construct graphic displays that will allow school faculty to readily identify patterns in the results of standardized assessments. Chapter 4 explains how to dig into student work, first in a single data source and then in other data sources, with the goal of identifying and understanding a student learning problem. Chapter 5 shows how to examine instruction in order to understand what current practice looks like and how it relates to effective practice for the student learning problem.

Act is about what to do to improve instruction and to assess whether the changes put in place have made a difference. Chapter 6 describes the tasks involved in designing an effective action plan. Chapter 7 addresses planning a process to assess whether students are learning more. A key message is that the assessment strategy and the action plan should be developed at the same time. Chapter 8 describes the key tasks involved in making an action plan come alive in classrooms, and in assessing implementation and effectiveness along the way. Chapter 9 describes steps school district central offices can take to support school-based educators' efforts to make constructive use of student assessment results. It is designed to be a resource for school superintendents and other district leaders committed to helping schools become "data wise."

The Data Wise Improvement Process

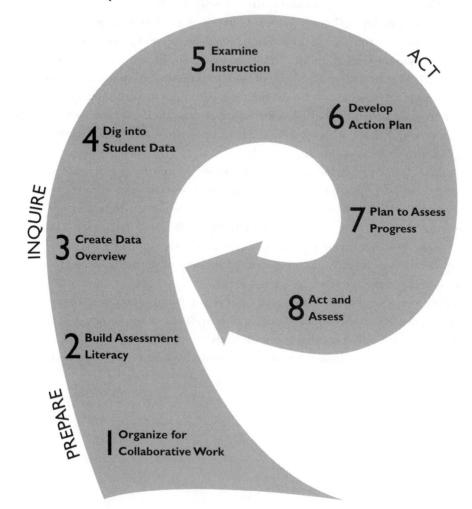

5 Examine Instruction

ACT

6 Develop Action Plan

4 Dig into Student Data

INQUIRE

7 Plan to Assess Progress

3 Create Data Overview

8 Act and Assess

2 Build Assessment Literacy

PREPARE

1 Organize for Collaborative Work

WHY START WITH HIGH-STAKES TESTS?

Although this book shows schools examining many types of evidence on student achievement, chapters 2 and 3 focus on lessons for examining student performance on externally imposed tests, such as state-mandated standardized tests or district-required tests of basic competencies. One reason to start here is that under NCLB and state and district accountability systems, schools are responsible for improving students' scores on these assessments. By looking carefully at what students are doing well and not so well on these tests (keeping in mind that there are often many possible explanations for poor performance on any given question), educators can begin to see connections between what they are doing in the classroom and how students are performing on external assessments.

Another reason for starting with results of externally imposed exams is that all faculty members recognize them as important to their school, whether they like them or not. In places like Franklin High, school leaders are often searching for ways to get teachers to really communicate with colleagues from other departments and grade levels.

A final reason for beginning with results on externally imposed tests is that by their very nature, these exams offer a measure of student achievement that is independent of the judgments of the teachers within the building. Although we do not dispute the argument that teachers are in the best position to understand their students' performance, having an external checkpoint against which to measure students' skills can catalyze fruitful discussions about standards.

Of course, how much educators can learn from the results of externally imposed standardized tests depends on the quality of the tests and on what information about results is made available. More can be learned from results on tests that are tightly aligned with state learning standards than from off-the-shelf tests used across the country. More can be learned when educators can see individual questions and responses or subscores indicating the degree of mastery of particular skills than when they only have an aggregate score for each student.

A central premise of this book, therefore, is that it is important to examine a wide range of data, not just results on standardized tests. Indeed, we will show that an analysis of standardized test results raises more questions than it answers. Examining other types of evidence on students' skills and knowledge is needed to answer these questions.

HOW TO USE THIS BOOK

Every chapter focuses on particular tasks school leaders face, tools to accomplish these tasks, and lessons from schools that have done this work. The book ends with references that readers can consult for more specialized knowledge on particular topics, and a few protocols to use to structure conversations.

To bring alive the descriptions of these tasks, we have woven vignettes from two case study schools throughout the book: Franklin High School, with students in grades 9-12, and Clark K-8 School, with students in kindergarten through grade 8. Both of our case study schools are working to improve student learning, not simply to improve test scores. Clark faces the challenge of how to build a sense of urgency for continuous improvement, rather than to accept as satisfactory the moderately strong performance most of its students show on standardized tests. Franklin High School faces a different, very difficult challenge: how to respond constructively to the enormous pressure to reduce dropout rates and failure rates on the state graduation exam. Each chapter describes the choices and challenges these schools face at each step of their respective journeys and illustrates the "messiness" of applying the improvement process in practice. When we need to provide a broader range of responses than these two cases can offer, we supplement our examples with brief descriptions of approaches taken by other schools we have worked with.

For leaders relatively new to the process of using data, we recommend skimming the whole book first and then working through the chapters sequentially with a group of committed faculty. In a sense, each chapter can be read as a "to-do" list of the tasks that will help move the work forward. By following the progress of the two case study schools as they work their way around the improvement cycle, your group will see how other schools handle these tasks. By using the protocols, exercises, and templates offered in the chapters, you should find it relatively straightforward to plan effective faculty meetings on each topic.

For school leaders with considerable experience in using data, it may not be necessary to follow the chapter sequence. Each chapter is designed to stand alone, allowing practitioners to focus on learning strategies that deal with the parts of the process that they find most challenging. Alternatively, school leaders can pick up this book at the point in the cycle where they find themselves, knowing they eventually will work their way around the entire circle.

District-level or independent professional developers and graduate school faculty may find this book useful in planning a year-long course that addresses one chapter per month. In our experience, schools learn a lot by working through the material in a particular chapter on their own and then coming together with people from other schools to share their work, discuss their concerns, and receive technical and moral support from instructors. School leaders are often energized by opportunities to show their school's work to colleagues from other schools and relish the chance to borrow good ideas.

For central office personnel and others who want to learn more about how to support school-level improvement, we recommend reading through the first eight chapters to develop an understanding of the challenges school-based educators face in attempting to learn from student assessment results. Then focus on chapter 9, which recommends actions district central offices can take to support school faculties' efforts to make constructive use of student assessment results.

Database designers can use the book to help think through the processes that their software needs to support. Test developers can use it as a window into what school-level people need from assessments—especially formative ones—and what they can do with results once they get them. Finally, policymakers at all levels can use this book to help understand how hard the work of using assessment data to improve schools is, how long it takes, and how worthwhile it can be.

SECTION I   PREPARE

5 Examine Instruction

ACT

6 Develop Action Plan

4 Dig into Student Data

INQUIRE

7 Plan to Assess Progress

3 Create Data Overview

8 Act and Assess

2 Build Assessment Literacy

PREPARE

1 Organize for Collaborative Work

1

ORGANIZING FOR COLLABORATIVE WORK

Kathryn Parker Boudett and Liane Moody

PRINCIPAL SANDY JENKINS'S HEAD WAS SPINNING AS SHE AND the Clark K-8 School's assistant principal, Bob Walker, headed back to the school after a three-hour training at the central office. It was the third week of August and the district had unveiled its new approach to school improvement plans. Responding to pressure from the state and federal governments to increase the use of student assessment data, the central office had designed a process that required schools to incorporate data analysis into their instructional planning. Sandy was alarmed to learn that to comply with the new policy her school would need to submit 14 separate documents.

"They sure dumped a lot on us," Bob remarked as they walked. "But don't worry ... it's not as bad as you think. I'm pretty familiar with the software they're asking us to use and I think I can run a bunch of analyses and get that improvement plan drafted before school even starts."

Sandy thought about this. As a first-year principal who was new to the building, she was glad to learn that Bob was willing to take one for the team so early on. It might be efficient in the short run to delegate this task to an eager administrator. Sandy's instinct, though, was that if all this planning was ever going to amount to anything, she would need to involve all of her staff in the process.

Principal Sandy Jenkins is struggling with a question that arises out of the recent policy focus on student assessment results: Is it better to tap a few individuals to become "data experts" and fulfill the reporting requirements alone, or to build a culture where the whole school participates in analyzing data and figuring out the implications for improving instruction? Across the country, school leaders face tough decisions about whether to take the relatively easy route of using data merely to fulfill external accountability requirements or the more challenging path of using data to help teachers become accountable to each other and their students.

Choosing the more challenging path increases the chances that your school will use data to inspire teachers rather than burden them and to illuminate deep issues rather than amplify superficial ones. Ongoing conversations around data are an important way to increase staff capacity to both understand and carry out school improvement work, but it takes effort to make sure these conversations are productive. The central message of this chapter is that there are specific steps school leaders can take to lay the foundation on which to build a collaborative learning process for school improvement.

In practice, there are a variety of ways schools can organize to effectively support ongoing conversations about student data. Deciding which approach is most appropriate for your school will require you to think creatively about how you can organize your school's time, people, and other resources in ways that permit teachers and administrators to engage regularly in meaningful discussions about student data. School leaders who make this happen have often described themselves to us as being committed to building a "data culture" or "culture of inquiry" within their schools. We have found that three activities in particular can support this kind of school culture. They are creating and guiding a data team; enabling collaborative work among faculty; and planning productive meetings. This chapter offers practical advice for engaging in these activities as you take your first steps on the challenging but rewarding path of using data wisely.

CREATING A DATA TEAM

Although your eventual goal is to promote ongoing discussions about data among teachers and administrators, the first step in getting serious about using data is to assemble a small group of people who will be responsible for the technical and organizational aspects of data work. The data team can help address what schools repeatedly tell us is the biggest barrier to using data—time. Having a few people responsible for organizing and preparing the data means that you can dedicate the full faculty's time to discussing the data. The data team's work may include managing the collection and organization of data from the state, district, and classrooms; creating graphic displays of this information; and teaching faculty members how to collect, organize, or display their own data. People who do this work are called upon to use a variety of skills: organizational skills for overseeing the coordination of multiple assessments; software skills for making the best use of technology; and people skills for interacting effectively with school staff and district personnel. Data team members need to have a clear understanding of teaching so that they know what kinds of charts and templates teachers will find most useful. And they must want to do this work and be given the time, resources, and support they need to do it well.

In our work with schools, we have seen a variety of creative approaches to establishing a data team, even when resources were limited. One school tapped its music and computer teacher to lead data-management activities. At another school, the principal "created" time for this work by having his intern from the local graduate school of education join the team and devote a substantial amount of her time at the school to helping the data team get off the ground. Another school's principal used a one-time grant to hire a consultant to create an assessment calendar and data-collection plan, and then train all of the school's teachers to collect and analyze data for themselves.

The Franklin High leadership team realized at its August retreat that managing data for the school's 1,520 students was a task too daunting to assign to any one individual. Instead, it created a data team responsible for overseeing the management of all assessments administered in the building. By committing himself to be a full member and tapping his director of instruction to lead the group, principal Roger Bolton signaled that he intended the data team's work to be central to the work of the school. Like many educators we have worked with, several Franklin educators volunteered to join the team because they could see that the school was finally committing to making constructive use of assessment data, and they wanted to play a role in this important transition. Roger expressed his understanding of the time commitment they would be making by exempting data-team members from other administrative responsibilities, such as supervising study halls and afterschool activities.

Even in cases where one person is willing to assume primary responsibility for data work, it is important that that person not work alone. Assembling a group of people, assigning responsibility for specific tasks, and planning how individuals will coordinate their efforts with each other and with the rest of the school helps send a message that using data in your school will be a collaborative effort. At the Clark School, which serves 450 students in kindergarten through eighth grade, principal Sandy Jenkins asked her assistant principal, Bob Walker, to assume the role of data manager. Bob had a strong interest and aptitude in the technical aspects of using data, and after some discussion agreed to focus his skills not on completing the work quickly but rather on building the capacity of Clark's teachers to use technology to analyze student assessment results. He agreed to work closely with two teacher leaders over the school year, one from the elementary grades and one from the middle school grades, to ensure that data expertise was not limited to school administration.

GUIDING A DATA TEAM

As a school leader, you are likely to find that the data team looks to you for guidance about how to focus their work. We have found three key tasks that school leaders can ask data teams to do early on that will set the stage for data work throughout the year: create a data inventory, take stock of data organization, and develop an inventory of the instructional initiatives currently in place in your school.

CREATE A DATA INVENTORY

When principal Sandy Jenkins announced at her first faculty meeting that this year's school improvement planning process would focus on learning from data, nobody clapped.

"Spending so much time on the state test just feels like such a waste," began a fourth-grade teacher. "Our school has one of the highest passing rates in the district; I don't understand what all the fuss is about."

"They may be passing all right," responded a seventh- and eighth-grade English language arts teacher, "but they're not exactly knocking the socks off the test either. But that is not what bothers me. The problem is that that the test gives such an incomplete picture of who our students are. It tells us essentially nothing about a lot of the things we all know really matter: how often they come to school, how they behave when they're here, what specific skills they're struggling with if they are new to learning English, whether they can write a decent term paper. We're not going to be able to figure out how to get our kids beyond simply passing if we don't take these things into account."

"Well then, let's broaden our definition of data," Sandy replied. "Somehow, I bet someone in our school has collected data on all of the things you just mentioned.

From what you've all told me, it seems there is an assessment of some kind being made nearly every week around here. I think part of the problem is that, as a school, we are not even sure what kinds of data are available to us."

Ask any teacher if she feels that her students are tested enough, or any school secretary if her school keeps track of enough types of student information. Enough? Most educators are likely to laugh! However, although a great deal of time is spent collecting data, most schools lack a big-picture view of exactly what data they have. A simple but powerful way of seeing this big picture is to create a data inventory like the one the Clark School data team created in Exhibits 1.1a and 1.1b.

Exhibit 1.1a

CLARK K-8 SCHOOL DATA INVENTORY: EXTERNAL ASSESSMENTS						
DATA SOURCE	CONTENT AREA	DATES OF COLLECTION	STUDENTS ASSESSED	ACCESSIBILITY	CURRENT DATA USE	MORE EFFECTIVE USE
STATE SKILL MASTERY ASSESSMENT	Reading; English Language Arts; Math	May (results in October)	Grades 3, 4, 5, 6, 7, 8	Intranet; Principal	Instructional Leadership Team analyzes data, looks for discrepancies and trends, and considers current curriculum and instructional practice with grade-level teams and curriculum coaches	Get all data on one sheet per child, including nonacademic data (student attendance, health issues, etc.)
OBSERVATION SURVEY	Reading	October January May	Grade K	Intranet; Teacher	Student benchmarking and retention decisions	Inform instruction
DEVELOPMENTAL READING ASSESSMENT (DRA)	Reading	September (January)(May); each trimester until at benchmark	Grades 1, 2, 3	Intranet; Teacher	Student benchmarking and retention decisions	Inform instruction
STANFORD 9		September	Grades 3, 4, 5	District	Advanced Work Class eligibility determinations	Item analysis
ENGLISH PROFICIENCY ASSESSMENTS	English	September; student entry	Grades K-8	Teacher; Principal	Student placement and accommodations	Track scores to find out time to proficiency
DISTRICT MATH ASSESSMENT	Math	January May	Grades K-8	District; Principal	Student benchmarking determinations	Discuss scores with students

Exhibit 1.1b

CLARK K-8 SCHOOL DATA INVENTORY: INTERNAL ASSESSMENTS						
DATA SOURCE	CONTENT AREA	DATES OF COLLECTION	STUDENTS ASSESSED	ACCESSIBILITY	CURRENT DATA USE	MORE EFFECTIVE USE
READING CHECKLISTS	Reading	January May	Grades K-1	Intranet; Teacher	Student benchmarking and retention decisions	Coached discussion about how results inform instruction
RUNNING RECORDS	Reading	January May	Grades 1-3	Teacher	Student benchmarking determinations	Grade-level analysis and conversation
WRITING SAMPLES	Writing	Formally in October and January; in school, about 1x per month	Grades K-8	Teacher	Looking at student work sessions between coaches and grade-level teachers; mini-lesson strategy development	Track rubric scores over time; create standard grade-level rubric
UNIT ASSESSMENTS	Math	Periodic when units are complete	K-8	Teacher summary sheets	Teacher use in identifying student math difficulties	Track data over time to ensure children gain necessary skills
OTHER STUDENT-LEVEL INFORMATION						
• Race/Ethnicity • English proficiency		• Disability • Retention		• Attendance • Socioeconomic status (reduced-priced lunch)		
Data Wish List						
• Date entered school		• Number of years in U.S.				

A data inventory provides a summary of all the types of data that are available in your school. We recommend that you maintain your inventory electronically. By updating and distributing the inventory regularly, you can ensure that it becomes a living document. You may find that putting this information together in one place helps your school develop a comprehensive picture of data resources and needs, which may jumpstart you into thinking about the kinds of questions that data can be used to answer.

It is helpful for a data inventory to include information about three types of data sources: external assessments, internal assessments, and other student-level information. External assessments are those required by external agents, such as district, state, and federal education agencies. Perhaps the most obvious example of an external data source you could include is your state-mandated educational assessment, such as the

State Skill Mastery Assessment listed at the beginning of the Clark School's table. Nationally developed and district-mandated tests such as the Developmental Reading Assessment (DRA) and the Stanford 9 Achievement Tests (SAT 9) are other common external assessments given in elementary schools. High schools may include the Scholastic Aptitude Test (SAT) and Advanced Placement (AP) exams, among other assessments, in their inventories. External assessments also include district-created subject tests, such as the mathematics exams included in the Clark School's inventory.

Internal assessments are instruments developed at your school, such as all-school writing prompts, science fair project assessments, end-of-unit tests, and quarterly grades. These assessments are often designed, collected, and scored by individual teachers or groups of teachers. Although often overshadowed in public importance by externally mandated tests, internal assessments can provide rich contextual information on students and are a valuable resource to include in your data inventory.

Other useful student-level information includes demographic and background data, such as that listed at the bottom of the Clark School inventory. Schools also often find it helpful to include a category for types of data they wish they had but do not currently collect. For example, teachers may want to know how long English-language learners have been living in the United States, or how many years each student has been enrolled at their school. Inviting teachers to contribute to a "data wish list "can encourage them to think creatively about what kinds of data could help them get a better picture of their students.

Once you've decided which data sources to include, you must also decide what descriptive information you should list about each source. The column headings of the Clark School inventory show types of descriptive information that can be particularly helpful. In addition to naming the data source, the inventory shows the content area of the source, dates of collection, and students assessed. Deciding how to fill in the final three columns—which identify who is allowed to see the data, what they are currently used for, and how they might be used more effectively—can get your faculty thinking critically about whether you are making the most of the information you have.

You may find that the process of putting together a data inventory leads your data team to create an assessment calendar. Such a calendar specifies in advance dates on which assessment administration, data collection, and data dissemination will take place and indicates who is responsible for recording, collecting, and compiling the data from each assessment. When you have a good handle on the kinds of information that will become available throughout the year and when, you may find it easier to begin planning how to use your data effectively.

TAKE STOCK OF DATA ORGANIZATION

The second task you can ask your data team or data manager to tackle early on is how to approach data collection and storage. Your data team can start by creating a data binder with sections organized by teacher or type of test. In most schools we have worked with, the principal keeps this binder at her fingertips so she can easily answer questions that come up throughout the year—from the central office, the community, or her own faculty—about how students are performing.

At some point in the year, your data team will need to think more carefully about the ways the information in this binder is presented. Because the task of reorganizing data is daunting and can seem like busy work when not undertaken with a clear purpose in mind, we do not recommend focusing on it early in the process. It is better to have your data team start by simply becoming aware of the possibilities for more organized assessment results. The team can tackle the actual reorganization once it is deeper into the improvement process and can see how this work will help achieve the school's goals.

We suggest that you and your data team answer the following two questions when examining the school's data organization. First, are you satisfied with the way you capture the information generated from each of your assessments? Second, are you satisfied with the way you capture information from multiple sources for each of your students?

When thinking about how your school keeps track of results from a particular assessment, you may first want to look at how you currently record such results. Is there is a better way to do it? One school we worked with decided to start by looking at the way it collected data from the midterm and end-of-year math and English tests required by the district. When it investigated how results from these assessments, which were delivered by interoffice mail in paper form, were used, it realized that almost no one used the results, except to assign course grades. In response, the school's data team got an electronic version of the test results, transferred the data to an Excel file, and then displayed them to show which skills students struggled with most. The new use and display of these data made it more likely that teachers could use the test results to understand which specific concepts students had mastered and which they had not.

If you decide to look at how your school captures information from a variety of sources about a particular student, your data team may find it helpful to develop a common data template for teachers. Such a template should be carefully designed so it is easy to fill out and easy to use to monitor student performance. For example, one school prepared an electronic student information template. To ease data entry, it provided spaces to enter assessment subtests in the order they are given. The template was designed to make it easy for teachers to track each student's progress over time. The school's intent was that teachers would use the information both to help them tailor instruction to the needs of individual students and to communicate those needs to parents, other teachers, and the students themselves.

DEVELOP AN INVENTORY OF INSTRUCTIONAL INITIATIVES

In carrying out the tasks just described, data-team members will begin to broaden their definition of the word "data "beyond the most common categories of information. You can ask them to broaden it further by exploring and cataloging the different kinds of instructional initiatives currently under way at your school. School improvement does not happen in a vacuum, and it is important to acknowledge what is already happening instructionally in your school before planning any improvements.

Instructional initiatives are programs that the school has consciously put in place to meet an instructional need. These initiatives can be implemented by the teachers of a particular grade or department or can be targeted at a particular student group. Sometimes the initiative pertains to the whole school. The inventory for Franklin High School presented in Exhibit 1.2 shows one way to capture this information in an easy-to-understand format.

Exhibit 1.2

FRANKLIN HIGH SCHOOL INVENTORY OF INSTRUCTIONAL INITIATIVES					
NAME OF INSTRUCTIONAL INITIATIVE	INTENDED TO BE IMPLEMENTED BY	FRACTION OF THE RELEVANT TEACHERS WHO ARE IMPLEMENTING 4=All (100%) 3=Most (>75%) 2=Some (25-75%) 1=Few (<25%)	AMONG IMPLEMENTING FACULTY, EXTENT OF IMPLEMENTATION 4=Completely 3=Mostly 2=Partially 1=Just beginning	EVIDENCE OF IMPLEMENTATION	OTHER EVIDENCE THAT WOULD BE HELPFUL TO COLLECT
COLLABORATIVE COACHING AND CLASSROOM VISITS	All teachers	3	4	Conversations with instructional coaches	Survey of teachers; classroom visits
FOCUS ON WRITING	All English language arts teachers	4	3	Whole school writing prompt	Student focus groups
WORKSHOP MODEL	All English language arts teachers	3	2	Teacher survey	Classroom visits; evaluations
DAILY JOURNALING	Homeroom teachers	Don't know	Don't know	Don't know	Class visits; student journals; student focus groups
RESPECT PROGRAM	Social studies teachers	2	Don't know	Informal conversations	Classroom visits; student projects
TEST PREP FOR STATE EXAM	15 teachers	4	4	Informal conversations	Classroom visits; curriculum overview

As Franklin's inventory shows, this document can be used to capture several types of information. The data team should begin by listing the names and target audiences of all the initiatives in place at its school. Many schools we have worked with are surprised to see how many programs they have, and by listing them all in one place they have discovered that some initiatives are redundant or contradictory. When the Franklin data team created its report, it was surprised to find many schoolwide initiatives devoted to literacy instruction, few to math, and none at all to improving instruction for students with strong academic skills.

The next step in creating an inventory is to estimate how many of the teachers who are supposed to be implementing the initiatives are actually doing so and to what extent. The purpose of this exercise is not to get at the "true" level of implementation of your programs but to start a conversation about how your school might think about measuring what is happening in classrooms. It is helpful for the data team to include in the inventory table the evidence it used to make its implementation judgments, as well as the evidence it would have liked to have had to make more accurate estimates. When developing an instructional initiatives inventory, data-team members are often surprised to discover how little they actually know about the extent to which the programs in their building are being implemented.

ENABLING COLLABORATIVE WORK

Although it may be desirable to delegate the technical work involved in *organizing* data to a small group, when it comes to *interpreting* data we have found that it is better to share responsibility among all teachers, and ideally among all members of the school community. When people are involved in analyzing and interpreting data collaboratively, they become more invested in the school improvement efforts that are generated out of those discussions. The more people involved in data analysis and interpretation, the more effective the resulting school improvement efforts will be. When planning conversations around data, the challenge is to find an effective way to give all faculty members a chance to make meaning of what they see. Two things that school leaders can do to support effective data discussions are to build strong teams and to create a schedule that allows for regular collaborative work.

BUILD A STRONG SYSTEM OF TEAMS

Having all staff members participate in a single ongoing conversation about data may be possible at smaller schools. For practical reasons, however, in larger schools it will be necessary to give staff members opportunities to discuss data in small groups and then report their findings to the larger school community. A good place to start is by deciding which of your existing school structures can become venues for data discussions and what new structures may be needed.

Principal Sandy Jenkins decided to have the Clark School's data discussions occur among the four well-established instructional teams in the school: one for kindergarten, first, and second grade, one for third and fourth grade, one for fifth and sixth, and one for seventh and eighth. In addition to these teacher-led teams, she asked the instructional leadership team (ILT), which included representatives from each grade-level team, as well as the principal and her assistant, to make data discussions a central part of their biweekly meetings.

Sandy also planned to revitalize a school-and-community team, a group formed to keep parents and other community members involved in the work of the school. She hoped this team would play an important role in deciding how to use data to inform school improvement. She summarized the relationships among the teams in a simple diagram (below) that conveyed a two-way flow of information between groups within the school.

Exhibit 1.3

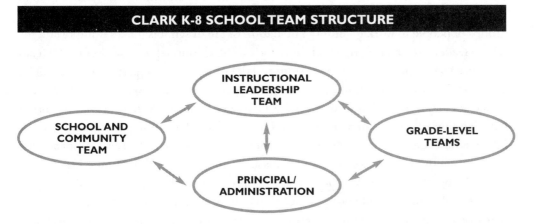

CLARK K-8 SCHOOL TEAM STRUCTURE

Creating diagrams like the one shown in Exhibit 1.3 can help clarify which groups will be looking at data and how the information learned from their conversations will be shared. Paying close attention to the connections between teams is necessary in order to ensure that everyone is involved in school improvement work. A key to creating a system of interlocking teams is to have every teacher be a member of at least one instructionally oriented team (such as a grade-level or departmental team), and then to have each team send at least one representative to the schoolwide team that makes decisions about instruction, professional development, and other matters.

As a school leader, the best way to keep in touch with the teams is by regularly sitting in on the various team meetings. However, you can use other strategies to keep you informed even when you can't be there. For example, if teams share their meeting minutes with you, you can stay abreast of the conversations that are going on, make sure that information is flowing freely between those teams and the school leadership, and note when teaching teams need assistance. When the principal in one school we've worked with reviewed the minutes from the weekly second-grade team meeting, she learned that the teachers were struggling to schedule an author's breakfast at which their students would display their work to their parents and the rest of the school. This information enabled the principal to step in and help the teaching team find a time that worked with the schoolwide calendar. Although this team was not facing a major problem, they were able to benefit from timely assistance from the principal and avoid becoming sidetracked by logistical issues.

CREATE A SCHEDULE THAT ALLOWS FOR REGULAR COLLABORATIVE WORK

Time is perhaps the scarcest resource in schools. And the only thing more difficult than finding time for an individual to concentrate on a particular task is finding time for groups of people to work together! The nature of life in schools makes it important for school leaders to plan how they will find time for these conversations to occur. The team structure you employ for data discussions will determine in large part what time will be used for this work. Incorporating data conversations into the work of existing team structures may require that team meetings be longer but less frequent. When discussing data, it is important to plan meetings that last long enough to allow participants to share information, generate understanding, and determine next steps. It is also important for the teams to think about data conversations as an integral part of their meetings, rather than as a separate activity that they engage in only periodically.

While data work should occur all year long, there are certain points when it is particularly helpful to have time for concentrated work. For example, some schools find data analysis most useful at either the end or the beginning of the school year, when conversations can meaningfully inform long-term instructional planning. Schools might also concentrate heavily on data analysis and discussion in January or February, when teachers can think about midyear adjustments. Some schools find that scheduling full- or half-day retreats with all or part of the faculty is an effective way to engage the staff in intensive data work at these times.

School leaders must make time in the yearly schedule for collaborative meetings. But how can you "make" time? We have seen a number of schools design creative schedules that allow groups of teachers to work together during the school day, which we refer to as common planning time, by being very deliberate in deciding when teachers will not have classroom responsibilities. One middle school designed a schedule in which teachers could meet during the school day by grade level on Mondays, Wednesdays, and Fridays, and by content area on Tuesdays and Thursdays. Teachers decided which day of the week to meet, and then met weekly with their grade-level and their content-area teams. At another school, the principal decided that teachers would participate in data discussions during afterschool professional development time with their departmental teams. A third school scheduled a 90-minute block every Friday morning for teachers to work together. Many schools use early release days for this work. While it may sometimes be necessary to arrange substitute coverage during class time, this approach costs teachers valuable instructional time with students and is best avoided.

PLANNING PRODUCTIVE MEETINGS

Once you've assembled a data team and set aside time for teams of teachers to meet, how do you know whether these teams will use their time well and work effectively? What can you do to increase the chances that good ideas will indeed arise in these meetings and that the ideas will lead to improvements in teaching and learning? Great conversations are often the result of careful planning and skillful facilitation. We have found the following four strategies to be particularly helpful in planning productive meetings: establish group norms, use protocols to structure conversations, adopt an improvement process, and "lesson plan" for meetings.

ESTABLISH GROUP NORMS

When team leader Inés Romero opened the first meeting of the Franklin High School data team, her colleagues were surprised to see her writing the word "norms" on a big piece of poster paper. As director of instruction, Inés had been leading meetings at the school for years. Was she suddenly going to try to change the way they did business?

"We're all used to having our test scores turned on us as a weapon," Inés began. "The press does it. The superintendent does it. Parents do it. But that's not how it's going to be inside these four walls. If we're really going to learn from our data, we are going to have to work together in ways we never have before. So I'd like us to start by agreeing on the kind of atmosphere we want to create for ourselves in our meetings.

"To get us started, I'd like to see us adopt a group norm of 'no blame,'" she continued. "When we look at the numbers, let's not use them to point fingers at each other. But I don't want to just stand here making rules; I'd like to hear from everyone." Inés passed out little pads of adhesive paper and asked each teacher to write down three norms they would like to see the group live by. By having teachers express their views this way, she freed them to make suggestions they might not have been comfortable making out loud. Then she asked team members to group the responses on the poster paper and opened a discussion about which of the recommendations teachers felt ready to adopt.

Looking at data in groups can be an intimidating process for teachers who worry that data will be used to blame them for weaknesses in their students' performance. Inés was beginning the important work of creating a productive environment for collaborative discussions of data by encouraging her team to set ground rules for how members would participate in discussions. Agreeing on norms like "no blame" is an essential first step in creating an atmosphere that supports productive data discussions. It is important to emphasize from the beginning that data will not be used to punish teachers, but to help them figure out how to teach their students more effectively.[1]

Another reason for setting norms is that many teachers have very little experience looking at data and may lack confidence in their ability to understand the numbers. They may resist participating in data discussions out of fear that they do not know how to analyze data the "right way." To deal with this issue, some schools we have worked with establish a norm that all team members approach their work in the role of learner. Understanding that there are no wrong answers and that discussions of data are opportunities to explore and learn can make teachers feel more comfortable. One principal we know emphasized the importance of understanding his teachers' individual learning needs with regard to data use. He provided one-on-one help to teachers who needed it, and strove to find leadership roles for those with significant knowledge. This differentiated support helped lower the barriers for teachers and emphasized the principal's willingness to make the process less intimidating.

USE PROTOCOLS TO STRUCTURE CONVERSATIONS

The strategy Inés used to start the norm-setting conversation is often referred to as a protocol. Protocols are structured ways of organizing interactions among group members, and we have found them to be an extremely effective way to ensure that data discussions are productive. In a fantastic book entitled *The Power of Protocols: An Educator's Guide to Better Practice*, Joseph McDonald and his colleagues offer brief descriptions of more than 20 protocols that educators can use to make their discussions more effective. Many additional protocol ideas are available on some of the education websites listed under Further Reading at the end of this book. Protocols can provide strategies for productively engaging in several tasks that are essential to data discussions, including setting norms, building group trust, coming to consensus, making decisions, and providing constructive feedback.

One protocol that we have used successfully with newly formed groups is called the Compass Points protocol.[2] This protocol, which takes less than an hour to complete, provides an excellent opportunity for members of a group to get to know one another while learning important information about their preferred working styles. In this protocol, individuals choose one of four characterizations that best describes their orientation when working on a team: "North—just get it done," "West—pay attention to details," "East—look at the big picture," or "South—take into account everyone's feelings." People with similar preferences work together to create a display that summarizes, among other things, the strengths and limitations of their style. When these groups report to the combined group, there are always many insights and many laughs. We find that in addition to breaking the ice, the protocol helps a group of people get to know each other and build tolerance for differences that might otherwise cause tensions in collaborative work.

While some people initially dislike both the "touchy-feely" and rule-bound aspects of protocols, in our experience most educators ultimately embrace them once they see how protocols can make groups function more smoothly. By providing structure, protocols lead to conversations that often deal with much deeper issues while maintaining a nonthreatening atmosphere. Throughout this book, we will show how the Clark K-8 School and Franklin High School use protocols to help with the various tasks involved in using data well. To make it easy for you to try these protocols with your own faculty, we provide citations for the protocols we mention and include step-by-step instructions for leading three of them in the Selected Protocols section at the end of this book.

ADOPT AN IMPROVEMENT PROCESS

Choosing an explicit improvement process to guide your work with data can be a powerful way of keeping faculty from feeling overwhelmed by what at first seems a monumental task. Organizing data work through an improvement process helps break it into manageable tasks on which teams can make meaningful progress.

As discussed in the introduction, this book is organized around an improvement cycle that we developed in the course of three years of working with schools. We have consistently found that this cyclical model of an improvement process helps educators get traction in the initially unfamiliar terrain of data work. When we work with schools, we make it clear that, in practice, school leaders generally do not work through a complete cycle in order, but instead revisit various parts of the process as reality demands. However, choosing a clear improvement process and locating data discussions within that process can be a great way to show your faculty how this work will affect whole-school planning and the everyday practice of the school.

One protocol we've developed to demonstrate the iterative nature of improvement work involves inviting participants to design their own improvement process, based on the steps we provide (see Protocol 1, Constructing the Improvement Process, at the end of this book). When it is time for groups to share their designs, there is always great variety. One group may have made a kind of staircase, while another created a wheel-like design with data analysis at the center. Almost all groups will have arrows going in many directions among the various steps of the process. In the discussion that accompanies their work on the project, educators explore the importance of each step in the cycle. When the groups see the variation in the posters created, they recognize that although no one way of describing this process is the "right" way, it is helpful to agree on some order of events to guide the work.

"LESSON PLAN" FOR MEETINGS

Data-team leader Inés Romero and principal Roger Bolton knew that if they were going to get teachers on board with the new focus on using data, the first faculty meeting of the year would be a great time to give the staff a positive, hands-on data experience. So they planned carefully how they would structure the meeting. They wanted to have everyone involved in looking at real data but didn't want to overwhelm them. They wanted to plan an activity that was manageable for the time available and would generate thoughtful discussion.

Inés and Roger agreed that they would ask the data team to create a handful of easy-to-read charts summarizing Franklin High School's performance on the state test. Then they would organize the faculty into small, cross-grade groups for the first half hour of the meeting to talk about what they saw in the data. Each group would share its major findings and record them on chart paper. In the last half hour they would have teachers follow a structured protocol for formulating questions about why the data looked the way they did. They hoped that if everything went according to plan, at the end of the meeting the faculty would have arrived at some consensus about the most pressing questions that Franklin High would need to address in the coming year.

In our experience, the most effective data meetings are as carefully planned as any good classroom lesson. For the schoolwide meeting described above, Inés and Roger planned ahead to ensure the faculty would work on an engaging task. For grade-level team meetings run by teachers or coaches, it is equally important that the person leading the meeting come prepared with a reasonable agenda, with handouts containing helpful data summaries, and with worksheets or other specific tasks that teachers are expected to complete before the end of the meeting. One school we worked with documented their strategy for structuring effective teacher-led meetings.[3] The structure provided by these "lesson plans" helps teachers stay focused on manageable tasks that may push the boundaries of their experience, but also give the group a powerful sense of accomplishment.

Another aspect of planning data meetings is to repackage data results so they can be easily understood by teachers and other school staff. Valuable meeting time is often lost when results are presented to large groups in formats that are difficult to interpret. Repackaging also helps focus the discussion on critical subsets of the assessment results. In our experience, presenting groups with too much data can lead either to teachers becoming overwhelmed or to very fragmented discussions as each teacher focuses on a different segment of the results. In chapter 3 we discuss the creation of a data overview—a display of standardized data results that explores a particular question— that demonstrates effective repackaging of data for collaborative discussions.

A FINAL WORD

Our experience working with schools has shown us that unless school leaders—principals in particular—are willing to champion the cause of analyzing data regularly and using the results to make decisions for the school, data work will not become a meaningful part of schoolwide reform. What does such "championing" look like? You can help data managers with their work. For example, obtaining the necessary data is sometimes a daunting task if not supported by the resources and clout available to school leaders. You can be present for many of the data discussions. By making yourself part of the conversation, you send the message that this work is central to your leadership mission and part of the decisionmaking process for the entire school. However, you may want to carefully consider what role to take in data discussions. Because the purpose of such discussions is to allow your faculty to interpret and construct their own meaning from school data, you will want to take care not to allow your own views to silence the group.

Finally, you can make sure that something happens as a result of all this talk. Once your faculty starts to see that the insights they gain from looking at data are used to help make decisions about how resources are allocated at your school and what gets done, you may find that the shift toward a "culture of inquiry" becomes easier and easier to make.

2

BUILDING ASSESSMENT LITERACY

Jennifer Price and Daniel M. Koretz

"WELL, IF WE'RE GOING TO GET SERIOUS ABOUT DATA," Clark School principal Sandy Jenkins thought to herself, "I'm going to need to get serious about understanding all these reports I get." She sat down with a stack of assessment results and the documentation that came with them. Within minutes, frustration set in.

"Apparent differences in scaled scores may not be statistically or educationally significant,"[1] one manual read. She then turned to another and was told that these results should not be used "to decide which instructional objectives should be taught at a certain grade level."[2] A third explained that "the results are most useful when they are considered in combination with other information about the student population and the educational system, such as trends in instruction, changes the in the school-age population, funding levels, and societal demands and expectations."[3]

With all this fine print, Sandy wondered how she will be able to guide her teachers in understanding what test scores mean and how they can be used appropriately. She knew there were plenty of assessment experts out there, but she didn't have the time or interest to become one herself. "If only someone would just tell me in plain English the key concepts that I need to know," Sandy mused, "then I could get on with finding out what these test results have to tell me about our kids."

When you look through the assessment reports for your school, it can sometimes feel as if they are written in a different language. So many terms, so many caveats, so many footnotes! As a school leader, how can you help your faculty begin to make sense of it all? Our experience is that if you develop a working knowledge of the key concepts described in this chapter, you will be in a good position to help your faculty develop assessment literacy.

A STYLIZED EXAMPLE

Assume that you confront the following challenge. As head of the English department at your high school, you have been asked to select a senior to send to a national tournament that tests participants' vocabulary skills. Because the prizes include large college scholarships, many students in your school would like to be selected. Of course, you want to select a student who has a particularly strong vocabulary to maximize the chance that the student you choose will win the tournament. You decide to use several different indicators to select the contestant, one of which will be students' scores on a vocabulary test. Designing an exhaustive test would be difficult because even a typical high school graduate has a vocabulary of more than 10,000 root words.[4] The only practical option would be to test the students on a small sample of words that they might know.

Let's assume that you have to construct the test and assume that you will need 40 words. You are given three lists from which to choose words. The first three words from each list are the following:

A	B	C
siliculose	bath	feckless
vilipend	travel	disparage
epimysium	carpet	miniscule

For each list, the words not shown are roughly similar in difficulty to those you see. It is obvious that one would learn nothing useful about an applicant's vocabulary skills from a test using the words in lists A or B. List A contains highly unusual, specialized words that few if any of the applicants are likely to know. Because all of the applicants would do extremely poorly on such a test, one would learn essentially nothing about the relative strength of their vocabularies. Conversely, list B is made up of extremely easy words that all high school seniors would know, which means that a test based on list B would similarly provide no useful information. Consequently, you would choose list C, which consists of words that are of middling difficulty. Some students would know any given word, while others would not. Only the use of list C would allow you to differentiate between the applicants with stronger and weaker vocabularies.

For the sake of this exercise, and for reasons we explain below, assume you decide to replace one word in list C, being careful to select another word that is on average as difficult as the original. For example, say you substitute "parsimonious" for "feckless." You quickly realize that this substitution may alter the ranking of applicants, even though the new word is no harder or easier than the old. One person might know "feckless" but not "parsimonious," while another applicant with a comparable vocabulary might know "parsimonious" but not "feckless."

PRINCIPLES FOR INTERPRETING ASSESSMENT RESULTS

This brief exercise illustrates a number of fundamental principles that are essential for the appropriate interpretation of students' test scores.

SAMPLING PRINCIPLE OF TESTING

The first and most fundamental of these principles could be called the sampling principle of testing. Most achievement testing is aimed at reaching conclusions about students' proficiency in a broad domain of achievement. In our example, the domain is vocabulary; it might be any other common subject area, such as sixth-grade reading or eighth-grade mathematics. You cannot possibly measure proficiency in such domains exhaustively because they are so large. You must instead create a small sample of the domain and measure each student's proficiency on that sample.

Because a test is not a direct measure of a student's degree of mastery of an entire domain, any conclusion you reach about proficiency in that domain is based on an inference from proficiency on the smaller sample. The quality of that inference—that is, the degree to which the inference is supported by performance on the test—is what is meant by validity. This is why measurement experts say that validity is an attribute of an inference based on test scores, not an attribute of the test itself. Even a test that provides good support for one inference may provide weak support for another. For example, an end-of-course algebra test may provide a solid basis for inferences about mastery of basic algebra, but it would not provide a valid basis for inferences about mastery of all of high school mathematics.

DISCRIMINATION

The choice of word lists illustrates a second principle, the importance of test items that discriminate. In the parlance of testing, "discriminate" means "differentiate" and has no negative implications. An item that discriminates is simply more likely to be answered correctly by students with a higher level of proficiency in the domain of interest—in this case, students with larger working vocabularies—than by those with lower proficiency. When you want to draw inferences about relative levels of proficiency, you need items that discriminate. There are other types of inferences for which discrimination is not important. For example, if one wants to know how many students have mastered a specific, discrete skill, an item that most students will answer either correctly or incorrectly and that therefore cannot discriminate may be acceptable. For inferences about variations in proficiency, however, one typically wants items that discriminate. Furthermore, one usually needs discriminating items in order to obtain accurate information about whether a student has successfully reached a performance standard. Using discriminating items does not create differences in proficiency, as some critics argue. Rather, discriminating items are used to reveal differences that alreasy exist. Whether that is good or bad depends on the inference the test is used to support. For example, if you simply want to know whether a class has mastered a list of new terms for a chemistry class, you may not be concerned about ranking students and you may want to include items that all or nearly all of the students can answer correctly. However, in the vocabulary example, and in all cases where scores are used to shed light on differences in students' performance, discriminating items are essential.

MEASUREMENT ERROR

The substitution of "parsimonious" for "feckless," as in the example earlier, demonstrates a third principle: measurement error. Measurement error refers to inconsistencies in scores across various "instances of measurement," such as multiple examinations. One source of measurement error, illustrated by our vocabulary example, is inconsistencies that arise when various forms of a test employ different samples of items. Another source of measurement error is inconsistencies in people's behavior over time. For example, a student might be better rested one day than another, or less distracted, or even ill. When students take a test such as the SAT more than once, their scores will typically vary as a result of both of these types of measurement error. When tests require scoring by people, a third source of measurement error is inconsistencies between individual scorers or by a single scorer over time. Clearly, measurement error can cause scores to be inconsistent.

RELIABILITY

The flip side of measurement error is our fourth principle: reliability. Reliability refers to the degree of consistency of measurement. A reliable measure is one that gives you nearly the same answer time after time, while an unreliable measure is inconsistent. If you have a cheap bathroom scale, for example, the chances are that it is not terribly reliable. You might appear to be two pounds under your target one time and at your target 30 seconds later, when you try again.

In our example, the substitution of "parsimonious" for "feckless" is analogous to your stepping on the scale twice: the two tests are two different "instances of measurement" that are intended to measure the same thing. Yet, the scores and ranking of candidates probably differ. If you asked the candidates to take 100 different tests with similarly difficult words, this difference would wash out over time. The test score is not systematically biased; it is simply variable from time to time. As a result of this variability, however, the score on one particular test is not necessarily a reliable measure of the candidate's true abilities. The key to understanding reliability is that the greater the measurement error, the lower the reliability. Clearly, you would want to design a vocabulary test that was quite reliable if applicants' scores were to play a large role in deciding who was chosen to send to the national competition.

SCORE INFLATION

Up to this point, this hypothetical example mirrors "low-stakes" testing—that is, testing without serious consequences for students or teachers, as is the case with much diagnostic testing. When testing has high stakes, however, we also have to consider how people respond to this pressure and what effect that has on the use of scores. As an extreme example, suppose that someone intercepted each of the applicants on the way to your testing session and taught them all of the words on your vocabulary test.

This example brings you face to face with the final principle: score inflation—that is, increases in scores that do not indicate a commensurate increase in actual proficiency. If someone taught the applicants the specific words in the tested sample, their scores would no longer tell you anything about the relative vocabularies of the applicants. Most applicants would get very high scores, regardless of their actual vocabularies. Real-world score inflation is often less extreme than this hypothetical case—which many people would consider simple cheating—but the principle is the same.

A FEW KEY ASSESSMENT ISSUES

In the rest of this chapter, we use "score" to mean a test score—that is, any form of score that describes a student's or a group's performance on a test, such as a percentage correct or an SAT score of 625. Test results are sometimes reported with scores for portions of the test (often called subtests) as well. For example, some achievement tests provide an overall math score as well as scores for several subtests, such as math concepts or computation. Sometimes people use the term "item score" to refer to performance on a single test item. To avoid confusion, however, we will never use "score" to refer to performance on a single item

ACCOUNTING FOR SAMPLING ERROR AND MEASUREMENT ERROR

To varying degrees, all assessment results exhibit measurement error, as already discussed, and they may contain sampling error as well. You are likely to encounter the concept of measurement error in test score reports, although it is not always labeled as such. For example, the Massachusetts Department of Education has reported scores from its Massachusetts Comprehensive Assessment System (MCAS) in the following manner:

Exhibit 2.1

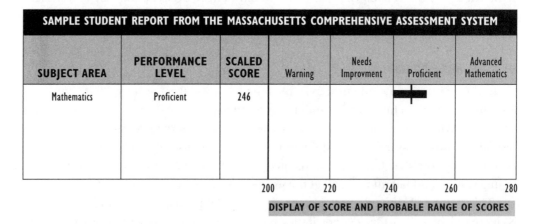

SAMPLE STUDENT REPORT FROM THE MASSACHUSETTS COMPREHENSIVE ASSESSMENT SYSTEM						
SUBJECT AREA	**PERFORMANCE LEVEL**	**SCALED SCORE**	Warning	Needs Improvment	Proficient	Advanced Mathematics
Mathematics	Proficient	246				

200   220   240   260   280

DISPLAY OF SCORE AND PROBABLE RANGE OF SCORES

The actual scale score (see explanation on page 37) this student received was a 246, which fell into the "Proficient" category. This scaled score is represented by the vertical line. The horizontal line (from 240 to 252) represents, in the words of the parents' test report guide, "the range of scores your child might receive if the tests were taken many times."[5] Because of measurement error, it would be a mistake to conclude that the student's score is precisely 246; perhaps it was too high this time, or too low. Therefore, the Massachusetts Department of Education has chosen to present a range of scores to illustrate the results one would get with repeated testing because of measurement error. In theory, the range could be of any width. If the range were made very wide, then the student's score would almost always fall within it. If the range were made very narrow—say from 244 to 248—the student, if tested over and over again, would often obtain a score outside of that range. Conventionally, for mathematical reasons, the range is most often wide enough so that if the student were tested repeatedly, 95 percent of the scores would fall within it; occasionally, however, you will find a narrower range that would encompass only about two-thirds of the scores the student would obtain.

Most people are more familiar with another kind of error that is analogous to measurement error: sampling error. While measurement error refers to inconsistency among multiple measures of a single person (or school, etc.), sampling error refers to inconsistency that arises from choosing the particular people (or schools) from whom to take measurements. For example, before every presidential election, we encounter polls showing that x percent of likely voters support a particular candidate, followed by a caveat such as "These results have a margin of error of plus or minus three percentage points." If one conducted the poll repeatedly, using a different sample of likely voters each time, the results would vary from one sample to the next just by chance because one sample might happen to include a few extra conservatives and another might include a few extra liberals. The margin of error is simply a way to quantify how much the results would vary from one sample to the next. Just as in the example of measurement error above, the "margin of error" is often the percentage point range that would include the results of 95 percent of polls taken from different samples.

Sampling error is an important consideration when considering aggregate scores from classrooms or schools, such as average scores or the percentage of students who reach the "proficient" standard established by the No Child Left Behind (NCLB) act. The cohort of students in any one year is often very different from those in previous years, and these differences among student cohorts cause scores to fluctuate substantially from one year to the next, even if the effectiveness of the school remains unchanged. This inconsistency tends to be particularly large when the performance of classrooms or small schools is described.

KEEPING TEST SCORES IN PERSPECTIVE

In the vocabulary example, an applicant's score was based on a small sample of words that represented a much larger domain. In many cases, the sample included in a test is not only small, but also incomplete in systematic ways. There are many important outcomes of education that are difficult to test. Therefore, while a well-designed test can provide valuable information, there are many questions it cannot answer. How well does a person persevere in solving problems that take a long time and involve many false starts? To what extent has a student developed the dispositions we want—for example, a willingness to try applying what she has learned in math class to problems outside of school? How well does the student write long and complex papers requiring repeated revision? People demonstrate growth and proficiency in many ways that would not show up on any single test.

For more than half a century, many measurement experts have warned educators and others to be wary of the limitations in using scores. These warnings are not an argument against testing but a reminder to use tests sensibly. In fact, some of the clearest warnings about these limitations were written by the authors of widely used tests. Scores from a single standardized test provide a specialized form of information that is very useful. For example, a score on a standardized test is comparable from one school to another because any given score has the same meaning regardless of the school a student attends. This is not true of course grades, or even grades on teachers' own tests. For this reason alone, scores on standardized tests are valuable, but they must be viewed as complements to other information about students' performance. Indeed, it is an explicit axiom in the testing profession that significant decisions about a student should not be made on the basis of a single score. The importance of examining multiple sources of information about students' performance is a theme that will be repeated in different ways, not only in this chapter but throughout this book.

DIFFERENT WAYS OF REPORTING PERFORMANCE

Performance on tests is reported in many ways, and the various forms of reporting sometimes seem to offer different pictures of student achievement. Each way of reporting also has its own advantages and disadvantages. Therefore, understanding some of the most common ways of reporting is critical to learning useful lessons from student test scores.

The simplest way to report performance is with a raw score, which is simply a count or percentage of credits achieved on a test. This is the most common way to report internal assessments; all students are familiar with classroom tests that are graded in terms of the percentage of possible credit. Raw scores seem simple, but they are difficult to compare and interpret because they depend on the difficulty of the particular set of items, included on the test. In other words, students with any given level of proficiency will get a higher raw score—number or percentage correct—if the test contains easy items, and a lower raw score if harder items are used. This is a common issue for teachers in schools in which the percentage correct is traditionally a cut score for a letter grade—for example, 90 percent or better gets an A. Teachers who grade this way can easily make some B students into A students (or vice versa) by changing the difficulty of their classroom tests. The same issue arises with external tests. Even if the developer tries to keep the difficulty of items consistent, they are likely to vary from test to test, causing misleading differences in raw scores.

Because raw scores are difficult to interpret without knowledge of the difficulty of the specific items on a test, performance on standardized tests is usually reported in terms of one or more types of scale scores, which we describe in more detail below. Even though the results of any test can be reported using many different types of scales, the scales emphasized in reporting performance should be related to the purposes of the test. We will next describe the main types of tests that are now in widespread use and then describe the types of scale scores often used to report results from those types of test.

NORM-REFERENCED TESTS

Of the tests we consider here, the oldest type comprises major, commercially prepared national achievement tests such as the Iowa Test of Basic Skills (ITBS), Stanford 9, and the Terra Nova. These tests are all norm-referenced tests (NRTs), which are tests that are designed to describe performance—often the performance of individual students, but in some cases that of schools, districts, states, or even countries—in terms of a distribution of performance. With an NRT, each person's (or school's) performance is reported in comparison to others. For example, the performance of a student would be reported in terms of how that student's performance compares to the distribution of performance of a sample of students nationwide. The group to which an individual is compared is called the norm group.

The simplest norm-referenced scale is the percentile rank, often abbreviated PR, which is simply the percentage of students in the norm group performing below a particular student's score. Thinking back to our vocabulary example, suppose a norm group took the test before you administered it to the candidates. Imagine further that 75 percent of the norm group answered fewer than 24 of the 40 questions correctly. All students who answer 24 items correctly (60% correct as a raw score) would be assigned a percentile rank of 75. Note that the percentile rank is not tied to the percentage correct. The percentile rank tells you where a student stands, but only relative to a specific comparison group taking a specific test. In our hypothetical example, the norm group includes all students taking the test, but it usually would be a nationally representative group or some other group chosen as a reasonable standard for comparison. When the comparison group is a nationally representative group of students, the percentile rank is often called the national percentile rank and is often abbreviated NPR.

Exhibit 2.2

AN IOWA TESTS OF BASIC SKILLS (ITBS) SYSTEM PROFILE[1]

	Grade: 1
	Level: 7
System: DALEN COMMUNITY	Form: K
Norms: SPRING 1992	Test Date: 03/93
Order No.: 000-A33-76044-00-001	Page: 91

SS=Avg Standard Score   Avg N Att=Average Number Attempted
GE=GE of Avg SS   Avg %C=Average Percent Correct
NCE=Avg Normal Curve Equivalent
NPR=PR of Avg SS: Nat'l Student Norms (▬▬▬▬)

TESTS N Tested = 255	SCORES					National Percentile Ranks							
	N	SS	GE	NCE	NPR	Low 1	10	20	Average 30 40 50	60	High 70		
Vocabulary	247	153.8	2.0	53.6	59								
Reading Comprehension	247	153.6	2.0	52.6	59								
Reading Total	247	153.7	2.0	52.8	58								
Listening	247	152.7	1.9	53.5	58								
Language	247	158.7	2.3	57.7	70								
Language Total	247	155.7	2.1	56.0	64								
Math Concepts	247	153.0	2.0	54.7	59								
Math Problems	247	151.0	1.9	50.7	53								
Math Total	247	152.0	2.0	52.6	55								
Core Total	247	153.8	2.0	53.6	58								
Social Studies	246	151.4	1.9	50.7	54								
Science	246	149.5	1.8	49.9	49								
Sources of Information	246	158.2	2.2	62.6	74								
Composite	246	153.5	1.9	54.1	60								
Word Analysis	247	155.8	2.2	54.3	62								
Math Computation	247	150.0	1.8	50.1	50								

[1] H. D. Hoover et al., *Iowa Tests of Basic Skills Interpretive Guide for School Administrators* (Chicago: Riverside, 1994): p. 102, Forms L and K, Levels 5-15.

For example, the first line of the ITBS report in Exhibit 2.2 indicates that first-grade students of the hypothetical Dalen County scored on average at the 59th percentile rank (NPR) on the ITBS vocabulary test. This result means that the average first grader in Dalen County scored higher than 59 percent of the students who comprised the nationally representative norm group.

The main advantages of the percentile rank are that it is familiar and easy to explain. The main drawback is less obvious: Any given amount of improvement in performance can translate into varying changes in percentile ranks. Typically, most students have scores near the average, and a much smaller percentage have very high or very low scores. Therefore, a student near the average who makes a given amount of progress—for example, answering an additional three items correctly—will "pass by" many students, simply because many students have scores similar to hers. As a result, her percentile rank will increase substantially. In contrast, a student with a very high or very low score who answers an additional three items correctly will "pass by" fewer students because there are fewer in that range of scores. Consequently, her percentile rank will increase less.

CRITERION-REFERENCED TESTS

A second type of test is a criterion-referenced test (CRT). A CRT is meant to determine whether a student has mastered a defined set of skills or knowledge. In the most common usage, CRT refers to a test that measures whether a student has reached a preestablished passing level, often called a cut score. For an example of a CRT, think back again to our vocabulary example. If the English department chair decides that she will only consider students who score 35 or above on the test, it is no longer important whether a candidate scores 40 or 35. In either case, the candidate has passed. In this instance, the vocabulary test does not rank students and serves only to differentiate those who passed from those who failed. The most important examples of CRTs are the minimum-competency tests that many states and districts have imposed as graduation or promotion requirements.

STANDARDS-REFERENCED TESTS

The newest type of standardized assessment is most often called standards-referenced or standards-based test (SRT). SRTs are developed by specifying content standards (what students should know and be able to do) and performance standards (how much of this content they are expected to know and be able to do). In terms of reporting, SRTs are very much like CRTs, except that in most instances three or four different performance levels are specified. (The NCLB accountability statute specifies several performance levels, but the accountability system uses only one, which in the statute is called "proficient.") For example, Massachusetts' MCAS assessment sets three performance standards and establishes four ranges of performance: "Warning or Failing," "Needs Improvement," "Proficient," and "Advanced." The primary forms of reporting for these tests (although not necessarily the only ones) are reports that show the performance range into which an individual student falls and those that show the percentage of students who exceed one of the performance standards. For example, the parent receiving the report in Exhibit 2.1 is told that that her child scores in the "Proficient" range. (NCLB requires that schools and states report performance in terms of the percentages of students reaching or exceeding the proficient standard.)

With a standards-based scale, information about performance within the ranges is not reported. For example, a student who improved from near the bottom of the "needs improvement" range to near the top of that range—a very large difference in many cases—would show no improvement. On the other hand, a student who progressed a very small amount but crossed a performance standard would be shown as having improved. Some states respond to this problem by reporting performance in an additional form. For example, some states use a scale score such as the one reported in Exhibit 2.1. However, to the extent that educators, the press, and policymakers rely on the standards-based scale itself—a common practice today—information about differences in performance between any two standards is obscured.

Standards-based scales have other limitations. The levels at which the standards are set depend on many factors, including the judgment of the panels assembled to set them, the particular method used to set them (there are many), and sometimes the characteristics of the test, such as the difficulty of items and the mix of item formats.

KEY OBSERVATIONS ON REPORTING STANDARDS

In practice, performance on any one of the types of tests described in Exhibit 2.3 may be reported in several ways, and the reporting is not entirely predictable from the type of test. For example, some commercial test companies have added performance standards to their NRTs, giving their customers the option of receiving both standards-referenced and norm-referenced reporting from a single NRT. In many cases, states construct scales for their SRTs that are very similar to those used with NRTs, and these scales are sometimes reported.

It is important to keep in mind that some of the scales that are used to report student scores are necessarily arbitrary. For example, there is no particular reason why the top score is 36 on the ACT and 1600 on the old SAT I (2400 on the new SAT I first administered in 2005). The test companies could have chosen any other numbers.

There are two important implications of this arbitrariness, however. First, a given score does not necessarily have the same meaning across different tests or even among the different subjects of a single test. Clearly, a 36 does not have the same meaning on the ACT as on the SAT (for which the scale does not even go that low). Typically, however, the scale is fixed so that a given score in one subject on a single test has a similar meaning from one year to the next.

Something is required to give meaning to arbitrary scale scores. In some cases, experience is enough. For example, teachers in high schools know that an SAT I score of 1550 is very high because experience has shown that these scores are rare, and anyone who has experienced with college admissions knows that this is a score that would make a student competitive at the most selective colleges.

In most cases, test authors don't rely only on experience, but instead take other steps to address the arbitrariness of scales. One common approach is to rely on norm-referenced reporting. If a student's scale score on an NRT puts her at the 95th percentile rank nationally, then we know her performance has been very good. Similarly, how does one know whether Minnesota's mean scale score of 288 in eighth-grade mathematics on the 2000 National Assessment of Educational Progress, or the finding that 40 percent of its students scored at the "Proficient" level or better, is good? One indication is state norms: Minnesota scored at the top of the distribution of all states participating in that assessment.[6]

Exhibit 2.3

TEST TYPE COMPARISON		
TYPE OF TEST	**DEFINITION**	**EXAMPLES**
NORM-REFERENCED TEST (NRT)	A test that describes performance of one unit (student, school, etc.) in terms of its relationship to a representative distribution of performance (norm group)	ITBS, Stanford 9, Terra Nova
CRITERION-REFERENCED TEST (CRT)	A test that is designed to determine if a student has mastered a defined set of skills/knowledge	Minimum competency tests
STANDARDS-REFERENCED OR STANDARDS-BASED TEST (SRT)	A test designed to measure a student's level of performance on predetermined content standards	Most current state-mandated testing programs

DEVELOPMENTAL SCALES

Educators and parents often want to trace a student's development as he or she progresses through school. Scales for this purpose are called, logically enough, developmental scales or "vertical" scales. An example of a developmental scale is grade equivalents (GEs), which are developmental scores that report the performance of a student by comparing the student to the median at a specific stage. For instance, a 3.7 grade equivalent represents the median performance of a student in the seventh month of third grade, so a third grader scoring 3.7 is typical, while a third grader scoring 4.3 is more than half a year above average. (There are ten academic months in a year on this scale.) Thus, the 2.0 GE reported as the average Vocabulary score for the Dalen County first graders on the spring ITBS in Exhibit 2.2 means that the average first grader in Dalen County is scoring at the median level of a second grader in their first month of school. Given that the ITBS is administered in the spring, this score would be considered to be slightly above the typical score. It is important to note that because the rate of growth changes with age, a difference of any given size—say, one GE—does not necessarily represent the same growth at different grade levels. For example, the difference between 3.7 and 4.7 does not represent the same performance difference as between 6.7 and 7.7. Unfortunately, even though GEs are relatively easy to interpret and explain, they have become unpopular and are rarely used.

A more common type of developmental scale, sometimes called a developmental standard score or a developmental scale score, reports performance on an arbitrary numerical scale. A fifth grader and a sixth grader who both scored 286 on a developmental scale on one test would be considered to have roughly the same level of proficiency, despite their being in different grades. For example, the average developmental scale score (SS) for Dalen County on the ITBS for the first-grade vocabulary test was 153.8 (Exhibit 2.2). This score does not tell you much unless you also know the median performance for a particular grade. In this case, the median performance for first graders is 150, so a score of 153.8 is slightly above what is considered typical. These scales are designed so that a given increase in performance (e.g., 50 points) has the same meaning at any level of the scale or grade level. Unfortunately, it is not clear that this goal is actually met, particularly for grades that are not adjacent.

When interpreting the results of a single test, it is often useful to obtain performance data from more than one scale. For example, a standards-referenced report of school performance is essential information under NCLB, but reporting only in terms of standards has numerous limitations, such as the lack of information such reports provide about progress within a performance range. Therefore, it is often useful to supplement this standards-referenced information with other types of reporting. Unfortunately, not all schools will have the same information available to them. Some states provide scale scores along with some types of benchmarks—in some cases, normative information—that help school leaders interpret the scale scores. Some states provide percentile ranks as well. Because different states provide different information, educators need to explore the options that are available to them.

Exhibit 2.4

SCORE TYPE COMPARISON		
TYPE OF SCORE	**DEFINITION**	**EXAMPLE**
RAW SCORE	A simple count or percentage of the credits achieved on the test	Classroom tests scored as percentage correct
PERCENTILE RANK	The percentage of students a given student outscores	SAT mathematics—a score of 700 = 95th PR[1]
CUT SCORE	The score needed to reach a predetermined passing level	Raw score required to pass a minimum-competency test
PERFORMANCE LEVELS	A number of levels that demonstrate a range of performance	MCAS—Warning or Failing, Needs Improvement, Proficient, Advanced
GRADE EQUIVALENTS	Developmental scores that report the performance of a student by comparing the student to the median at a specific stage	ITBS—a GE of 3.7 represents the median performance of a student in the seventh month of third grade
DEVELOPMENTAL SCALE SCORE	Developmental scores that report the performance of students in different grades on a single numerical scale	ITBS Form K—176 is the developmental scale score corresponding to a GE of 3.2 in reading[2]

[1] *SAT Program Handbook: 2004-2005* (New York: College Board, 2004).
[2] H. D. Hoover et al., *Iowa Tests of Basic Skills Interpretive Guide for School Administrators* (Chicago: Riverside, 1994): p. 74.

TRADING OFF DETAIL FOR RELIABILITY

Typically, performance on external tests is reported at many levels of detail. At one extreme is the total score for the whole test. Performance at this level can be reported in terms of any of the scales noted above. At the other extreme, some tests report performance on individual test items. In between there may be several intermediate levels of detail such as subtest scores. Each subtest typically comprises many test items, and performance on the subtests is often presented in terms of the scales noted above. At a finer-grained level of detail, some tests will report results on small clusters of items that depend on similar knowledge or skills, as shown on the ITBS report in Exhibit 2.5. Most often, as on the ITBS report, performance on these small clusters is not reported in terms of scale scores because there is too little information to create a reasonable scale. It is reported instead in terms of simple statistics, such as the percentage of items in the cluster answered correctly.

For purposes of diagnosis and instructional improvement, most educators want more detail rather than less. Knowing that a class does poorly in math, or even in "math computation," provides limited guidance about how to improve its performance. On the other hand, knowing that many of the students in the class have difficulty with the concept of place value provides a clear starting point for planning improvement.

So why not just use the most fine-grained detail available from a test? As in many aspects of assessment, there are trade-offs—in this case, between detail and reliability. Although finer-grained levels of detail are instructionally more useful, because fewer items are used in reporting performance the results will also be less reliable. For example, looking at an ITBS report similar to the one in Exhibit 2.5, a school leader would be more confident that the test reliably assessed students' performance on "Number Systems and Numeration" (based on nine questions) than their performance on "Estimation" (based on one question). When you opt for a finer level of detail in order to obtain more useful diagnostic information, you simultaneously opt for a measure that is less consistent and has a higher probability of being misleading because of measurement error. As we discuss below, one way to deal with the limitations of information from a single test is to combine it with other information about performance. The finer-grained the information you take from the test and the fewer items it reflects, the more important such additional information becomes.

At the extreme, some states encourage teachers to examine performance on individual items. A single item is a risky basis for inferring what students can and cannot do. To clarify this, it is necessary to distinguish between using a single item to learn about an individual student and relying on it to help describe the performance of a class, school, or other group.

Exhibit 2.5

	GROUP ITEM ANALYSIS FOR FIRST GRADE IOWA TESTS OF BASIC SKILLS (ITBS)[1]						
Item No.	MATH CONCEPTS	Item Count	ClassAvg %C N=21	Building Avg %C N=139	System Avg %C N=247	Nat'l Avg %C	Diff (Class Minus Nat'l)
	NUMBER SYSTEMS & NUMERATION	9	76	68	68	65	+ 11
1	Compare & order		95	89	91	86	+ 9
5	Compare & order		90	83	80	72	+ 18
7	Compare & order		86	72	75	74	+ 12
12	Place value		90	90	89	88	+ 2
15	Compare & order		76	68	67	67	+ 9
17	Place value		90	83	84	71	+ 19
22	Compare & order		38	31	30	30	+ 8
26	Properties		48	35	34	32	+ 16
29	Compare & order		67	65	62	62	+ 5
	WHOLE NUMBERS	3	84	85	83	82	+ 2
2	Reading and writing		81	82	64	95	- 4
6	Reading and writing		100	93	89	93	+ 7
11	Relative values		71	79	75	68	+ 3
	GEOMETRY	4	82	86	84	80	+ 2
3	Geometric figures		90	93	92	91	- 1
14	Properties, patterns and relationships		76	82	78	72	+ 4
19	Geometric figures		67	74	73	67	0
25	Properties, patterns and relationships		95	95	93	89	+ 6
	MEASUREMENT	4	88	88	88	82	+ 6
9	Appropriate units		100	98	97	95	+ 5
13	Estimate measurements		81	80	81	72	+ 9
16	Length, distance, temp, wt, vol		95	97	95	81	+ 14
21	Estimate measurements		76	76	78	79	- 3
	FRACTIONS & MONEY	4	79	63	63	57	+ 22
10	Representation		90	71	72	68	+ 22
23	Representation		38	24	27	22	+ 16
24	Representation		95	82	79	85	+ 10
27	Relative values		90	76	74	54	+ 36
	NUMBER SENTENCES	4	75	71	67	67	+ 8
4	Solving sentences		95	86	84	79	+ 16
8	Symbols		86	89	88	91	- 5
18	Variables		57	51	47	48	+ 9
20	Variables		62	58	49	51	+ 11
	ESTIMATION	1	29	46	49	47	- 18
28	Standard rounding in context		29	46	49	47	- 18

[1] H. D. Hoover et al., *Iowa Tests of Basic Skills Interpretive Guide for School Administrators* (Chicago: Riverside, 1994): p. 88.

There are two basic reasons why it is risky and often seriously misleading to rely on a single item to draw conclusions about a single student. One reason is the measurement error already discussed—that is, students' performance often varies markedly from one item to another, even when the items are intended to measure the same thing. A second reason is that more than one skill is needed to answer many items correctly, particularly on some modern assessments that deliberately aim for more realistic, and therefore often more complicated, items. When a student answers one item incorrectly, it is often not clear whether she would answer another similar item incorrectly, or which of several skills she has not learned.

When looking at the performance of a class or another group, the problem of measurement error is lessened, but the second problem remains because there are often several possible explanations for poor performance on the item. Therefore, the best way to use information about poor performance on a single item is to understand that such performance suggests possible weaknesses in students' knowledge and skills. Measurement experts would generally advise testing these possible explanations by looking at clusters of items that share the skill in question but differ in other respects. In many instances, however, you may find yourself without additional items you can use in this way. When you don't have additional items to rely on, you should take any conclusions based on a single item with a large grain of salt and look for additional evidence to test your hypothesis about the reasons for incorrect answers.

HOW DO YOU MEASURE IMPROVEMENT?

Schools and policymakers follow two very different approaches for using test scores to measure progress over time. The most common model, mandated by NCLB but widely used in state testing programs before its enactment, is called a cohort-to-cohort change model. In this approach, schools test a given grade (e.g., fourth grade) every year. To gauge progress, each year's scores for students in that grade are compared to the scores of the previous year's students in that grade. This approach compares one cohort of fourth graders to the previous cohort of fourth graders—hence the name given to the approach. This approach is shown for a hypothetical state in Exhibit 2.6. Average scores for each cohort of fourth graders are presented on a hypothetical developmental (or "vertical" scale). Exhibit 2.6 shows a typical pattern: rapid gains over the first few years of the testing program, followed by slower gains after several years.

Exhibit 2.6

RESULTS FROM A COHORT-TO-COHORT ASSESSMENT OF CHANGE

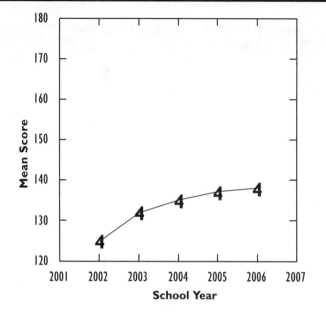

An alternative approach measures the gains shown by a given cohort of students as it progresses through school. This approach goes by various names, including "value-added assessment" and "longitudinal assessment." The value-added approach is illustrated for the same hypothetical state in Exhibit 2.7, using the same developmental scale. In Exhibit 2.7, a single cohort of students, those who were tested in the fourth grade in 2002, are followed as they progress through school. The same graph illustrates the scores of this cohort as its members were tested in fifth grade in 2003, sixth grade in 2004, and so on.

Each of these approaches has advantages and drawbacks. The cohort-to-cohort approach is simple to implement and allows schools to use grade-specific tests without worrying about grade-to-grade overlap or vertical scaling. It is designed to measure improvement in the performance of the school's students over time—from one cohort to the next—not its effectiveness in teaching any one cohort of students. On the other hand, the cohort-to-cohort approach has a "perpetual motion machine" flavor because it rests on the assumption that schools can just keep improving without limit. The problem with this assumption is clear if you consider a highly effective school in which students learn a great deal and in which that rate of learning is stable over time. Such a school would show up in a cohort-to-cohort gain system as showing no improvement over time.

Exhibit 2.7

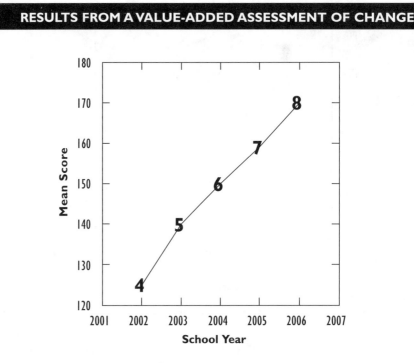

RESULTS FROM A VALUE-ADDED ASSESSMENT OF CHANGE

The cohort-to-cohort approach is also susceptible to biases caused by changes in the composition of the student population. For example, a school that is improving may show up as making no progress if it is faced with an influx of lower-scoring students, for example, students with limited proficiency in English. Estimates of change in a cohort-to-cohort change system are also highly susceptible to meaningless fluctuations that arise from differences among the cohorts entering school in different years. This issue is particularly true of smaller schools.

In contrast, the value-added approach is designed to measure directly what students learn while in school, which makes it an appealing option for many educators and policymakers. However, it too has its disadvantages. One is that comparing a student's performance across grades requires tests that can be placed on a vertical scale. This is possible only when the curriculum is cumulative across grades—as is the case with reading, but not high school science. Because the curriculum changes from grade to grade, these estimates of growth become increasingly questionable as the span of grades increases. These estimates are also highly susceptible to measurement error. For example, recent research suggests that value-added assessments can reliably distinguish classrooms in which gains are exceptionally large or small but do not reliably distinguish among most classrooms.[7]

STRATEGIES FOR INTERPRETING DATA

INTERPRETING SINGLE TEST SCORES

As discussed above, measurement error is one reason not to evaluate a student on the basis of only a score on a single test, but it is not the only reason to avoid using a single score in isolation. We all have had the experience as a student of a test not measuring our true competence in a particular subject area. As educators, we know that a student's situation is sometimes important to understand when viewing test results. Is the student learning disabled? Does the student suffer from test anxiety that depresses her performance on tests? Does the student show either much stronger or much weaker performance on other types of work than on tests? These are not examples of measurement error because repeated testing would not give you an average score that would be a more accurate indicator of the student's performance. However, they are factors that might cause a score, if taken alone, to be a biased indicator of the student's proficiency.

We suggest three complementary strategies for interpreting scores on a particular assessment, all of which involve use of additional information. First, look beyond one year's assessment results by applying the cohort-to-cohort change or value-added assessment approaches as explained above. While the two approaches provide different information, both are valuable in making sense of the most recent assessment results.

Second, compare your students' results with those of relevant students in the district or the state. For example, a principal might be concerned to see that only 64 percent of the tenth-grade students at her school scored at the proficient or the advanced level on the state English language arts test. However, discovering that the comparable percentages for tenth graders in the district and the state were 62 and 61 percent, respectively, would cause her to reassess her school's performance. Of course, such comparisons raise the question of "how good is good enough?" We will return to this question when we discuss setting goals in chapter 7.

Third, compare your students' results on the most recent assessment with their performance on other assessments. Following the advice in chapter 1 to conduct a data inventory for your school provides the critical information about what other data on student performance are available.

DETERMINING WHETHER DIFFERENCES ARE MEANINGFUL

Given the current high-stakes nature of many assessments, educators, parents, and policymakers are looking for meaning in even the smallest differences. Yet some of these differences may not represent any real change in student performance.

There are three reasons why small differences should not be given credence. As we have discussed, the first is sampling error. This error even affects large groups, such as the samples of roughly 2,500 students that were tested at the state level for the NAEP until very recently. If you look at the comparisons among states, you will find that many states with similar scores were rated not statistically significantly different. This result means that if different samples of students were chosen to take the test, the states could score the same as each other or the rank order might even change. The uncertainty resulting from sampling error is, of course, much greater in the case of individual schools, particularly small ones. The second reason, measurement error, is analogous, but it stems not from the sampling of people, but rather from the sampling of items on the test.

A third reason to be wary of small differences is that any given set of content standards could lead to a variety of different blueprints for a test. Different people may reach different conclusions about what specific content should be included and which formats should be used. Therefore, different tests generally provide a somewhat different view of performance. Individuals, schools, and even states and countries will show somewhat different performance on two tests that are designed to measure the same domain.

Although fully addressing these sources of uncertainty requires substantial knowledge of statistics, measurement, and the specific test, there are things you can do to guide your interpretation of assessment results. First, you will sometimes be able to find information about the types and extent of error. For example, score reports for individual students often provide some information about measurement error. Reports of group data often have information about which comparisons are statistically significant—that is, big enough that they would not likely arise from sampling or measurement error, and therefore are worth accepting with confidence. Even if such information is not reported, it is worth finding out if it is available.

Second, even in the absence of this information, you should be wary of small differences, including differences between groups or changes in performance over time. Differences that are sizable or that persist for some time should be taken seriously. Small differences, or differences that have appeared only in one time period (say, when comparing this year to last), should be taken with a grain of salt and, if small, should be ignored until more data are available to confirm them.

UNDERSTANDING "GAMING THE SYSTEM"

Some school leaders respond to the introduction of high-stakes assessments by figuring out how to game the system. Test-preparation firms have developed a profitable business by trying to teach people to succeed on specific tests, and some of their techniques rely on gaming the system rather than on building student mastery. In addition, numerous studies have found that when the pressure to raise scores is high, some teachers will engage in questionable practices to increase student test sores. For example, Exhibit 2.8 provides a summary of responses by teachers in Kentucky and Maryland to surveys investigating their responses to state testing programs.[8]

Exhibit 2.8

PERCENTAGE OF TEACHERS REPORTING QUESTIONABLE TEST-ADMINISTRATION PRACTICES IN THEIR SCHOOLS[1]		
TEACHER PRACTICE	**KY**	**MD**
Questions rephrased	36	27
Questions about content answered	21	13
Revisions recommended	21	14
Hints given or correct answer given	17	6
Answers changed	9	2
Helpful materials or posters in view	na	42

[1] D. Koretz, "Preparing Students for the MSPAP Assessments," in *Assessment-Based Educational Reform: A Look at Two State Programs, Part 2,* symposium presented at the annual meeting of the American Educational Research Association (Jessie Pollack, chair), New York, April 1996.

Another practice that many educators employ to inflate scores is reallocation, which refers to shifts in instructional resources among the various parts of a content area. Research has shown that when scores on a test are important to teachers, some will reallocate their instructional time to focus more on the material emphasized by the test and less on the material that either is omitted from the test—for example, all the words not included in our vocabulary test—or is emphasized less by it.[9] Just as reallocation transfers time among parts of the content area, it also reallocates achievement among them. Whether this reallocation inflates scores depends on which material gets more emphasis and which receives less. If teachers deemphasize material that is important for the inferences you and others base on the scores—that is, if they are an important part of the curricular domain (the 10,000 words) the test is supposed to represent—then scores will become inflated. This is true even if the material gaining emphasis is important. Scores will go up, but mastery of the domain will not. This is why having "a test worth teaching to," while desirable for many reasons, is not sufficient to protect against score inflation.

Research has shown that reallocation also occurs between subjects as a result of high-stakes testing.[10] Schools and districts feel the pressure to demonstrate improvement in tested subject areas, and some consequently reallocate instructional resources and time away from untested areas. As Exhibit 2.9 demonstrates, this often leads to a deemphasis on subjects such as science, social studies, arts, and health and fitness. When this occurs, a subsequent increase in math scores, for example, may truly demonstrate increased mastery of math material. Yet, this increase most likely comes at the price of decreased mastery of science and/or social studies material.

Exhibit 2.9

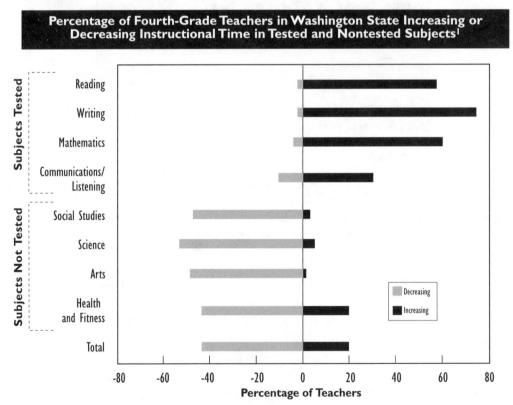

Percentage of Fourth-Grade Teachers in Washington State Increasing or Decreasing Instructional Time in Tested and Nontested Subjects[1]

[1] B. M. Stecher, S. I. Barron, T. Chun, and K. Ross, *The Effects of the Washington State Education Reform on Schools and Classrooms* (CSE Technical Report No. 525) (Los Angeles: National Center for Research on Evaluation, Standards, and Student Testing, 2000).

Several studies have shown that educators' responses to tests with high stakes result in substantial grade inflation. One relevant study examined performance in a large, predominantly minority, high-poverty district that by today's standard had a "moderate-stakes" testing program—although it carried no formal rewards or sanctions, the administration put a great deal of pressure on educators to raise scores. Through 1986, the district had used one standardized achievement test and had seen test scores rise. Specifically, in the spring of that year, the average third grader scored at a grade equivalent of 4.3 (4 years, 3 months)—fully half an academic year above average. This is shown by the first diamond in Exhibit 2.10.[11] The district then purchased a new, quite similar test, shown by the squares in Exhibit 2.10, and performance dropped to an average level. Four years later, the district's performance on the new test was again half an academic year above average. The researchers then administered to a random sample of classrooms exactly the same test that had been administered previously. They found that while performance on the new test had increased by half an academic year, performance on the old test had declined by the same amount, as shown by the diamond on the right in Exhibit 2.10.

Exhibit 2.10

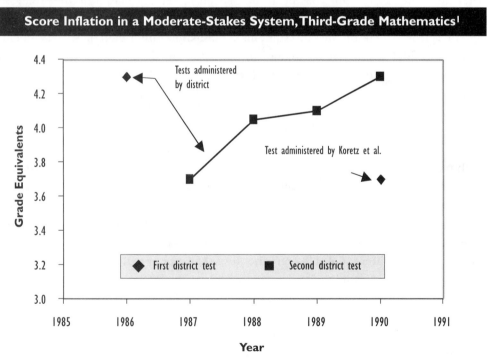

Score Inflation in a Moderate-Stakes System, Third-Grade Mathematics[1]

[1] Adapted from D. Koretz, R. L. Linn, S. B. Dunbar, and L. A. Shepard, "The Effects of High-Stakes Testing: Preliminary Evidence About Generalization Across Tests," in *The Effects of High-Stakes Testing*, symposium presented at the annual meetings of the American Educational Research Association and the National Council on Measurement in Education (R. L. Linn, chair), Chicago, April 1991.

Thus, regardless of the test used, students scored a half-grade equivalent lower on a test that was unexpected than on a test for which teachers had time to prepare. It does not appear that the gains in scores on the second test represent clear improvements in learning—as might occur if the second test were harder or if students learned new material on the new test without losing ground elsewhere. If that had been true, performance on the first test would not have declined. Rather, it appears that students and teachers substituted mastery of material emphasized on the second test for mastery of material emphasized on the first test. Achievement was transferred among material sampled from the domain for the two tests. Unless one could argue that the material from the first test that was deemphasized was unimportant to the conclusions parents and teachers drew about mathematics proficiency, this represents score inflation.

Similar patterns have been shown by a number of other studies.[12] Typically, gains on high-stakes tests have been three to five times as large as gains on other tests with low (or lower) stakes. In numerous cases, large gains on high-stakes tests have been accompanied by no gains whatever on lower-stakes tests.

To understand whether improved student scores are meaningful, educators need to determine whether teaching has been focused on increasing mastery rather than on changing scores. What does it mean to do this? There is no simple answer, but the general rule is to focus on the skills students should know rather than on specific details of the test. Students are not in school to learn how to score well on a specific test required by their state's department of education; they are there to learn the skills they need to be successful in subsequent schooling, in their later work, and as citizens. The criterion to apply as you prepare students for such a test is whether you believe the preparation will create general improvement or merely improve performance on the specific test. Teaching test-taking tricks (e.g., plugging in a formula rather than solving a math problem) fails to meet this standard. So does focusing on details of the particular test. For example, one secondary school teacher told us that she no longer bothers to teach her students about irregular polygons because her state's test only includes regular polygons. This is a short-cut that will generate higher scores but not a truly higher level of competence. If students are gaining mastery, then the improvement will show up in many different places—on other tests they take or in the quality of their later academic work—not just in their scores on their own state's test.

This book focuses on how to use assessment results to change practice in ways that make a long-term, meaningful difference for students. In some cases, school leaders will need to create cultural changes in their schools, provide new forms of professional development, and combat incentives to focus on the test rather than on the broader domains of skills and knowledge. We understand that often this means going against the tide by resisting the pressure to do whatever it takes to raise scores. During this process, it is necessary to monitor not only impediments to raising scores, but also practices that result in score inflation rather than meaningful improvement. As you will see in the following chapters, this work can be challenging and messy.

SECTION **II**   **INQUIRE**

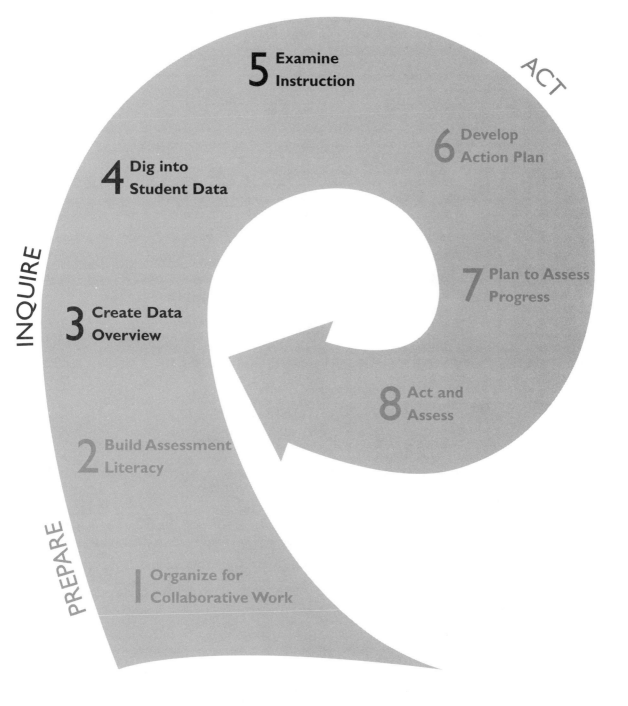

5 **Examine Instruction**

ACT

6 **Develop Action Plan**

4 **Dig into Student Data**

INQUIRE

7 **Plan to Assess Progress**

3 **Create Data Overview**

8 **Act and Assess**

2 **Build Assessment Literacy**

PREPARE

1 **Organize for Collaborative Work**

3

CREATING A DATA OVERVIEW

Shannon T. Hodge and John B. Willett

DATA-TEAM LEADER INÉS ROMERO AND PRINCIPAL ROGER Bolton had agreed that Franklin High School's first faculty meeting of the year would focus on the newly released results from the state assessment. They hoped to engage the faculty in a spirited conversation about what they saw in the data. However, when they got right down to it, deciding what data to present didn't seem so easy.

"I can tell you right now," Inés remarked as Roger held up a table packed with numbers, "we'll lose them right away if we stick something like that on the overhead."

"I know," responded Roger." But what do we show them? How do we turn this pile of paper into a story that people can follow?"

This chapter provides advice about how to construct graphical displays that highlight important patterns in assessment results, which can then be used to engage school faculties in constructive conversations about the meaning of those results. The primary challenge in constructing such displays is to direct the audience's attention to important patterns while respecting the limitations of assessment results as described in chapter 2. Other important considerations include deciding which of the many pieces of assessment data to display, how to display those data clearly and effectively, and how to start conversations around these displays.

This chapter has four major sections, each of which is organized around the tasks a data team would do to prepare for a faculty meeting on assessment results. The first section explains that a data team should begin by choosing the educational questions it wants to highlight. The second section emphasizes that the data team should prepare its displays by using a" simpler is usually better" approach. The third section explains that one good approach for stimulating faculty debate is to seek out and display interesting comparisons—for example, comparisons among students in important demographic groups, across yearly cohorts, or over time. The final section describes ways school leaders can use these displays to facilitate constructive conversations among faculty members.

DECIDE ON THE EDUCATIONAL QUESTIONS

Administrators like Roger Bolton often get their first glimpse of their schools' student assessment results in test-score reports, such as those displayed in the three panels of Exhibit 3.1. These reports present aggregate results from the 2005 administration of the State Comprehensive Assessment to tenth graders at Franklin High School. They show how Franklin High students were distributed across state-defined proficiency levels in the content areas of "English Language Arts" and "Mathematics." The form of these reports is very similar to the test-score reports used by many states and testing companies.

Exhibit 3.1

Distribution of Scores of Franklin High School Tenth-Grade Students across State-Defined Proficiency Levels on the State Comprehensive Assessment in English Language Arts and Mathematics

Panel A: Percentage of Students at Each Proficiency Level, by Subject Specialty and Cohort (Academic Year)

GRADE 10	ENGLISH LANGUAGE ARTS				MATHEMATICS			
	2002	2003	2004	2005	2002	2003	2004	2005
Advanced	1	1	2	1	2	6	5	2
Proficient	7	6	5	19	10	9	10	7
Needs Improvement	28	38	42	43	13	12	19	41
Failing	64	55	51	37	75	73	66	50
Total Students	414	425	417	423	417	430	422	425

Panel B: Number and Percentage of Students at Each Proficiency Level for School, District, and State, by Subject Specialty, 2005 Academic Year

GRADE 10	ENGLISH LANGUAGE ARTS						MATHEMATICS					
	School		District		State		School		District		State	
	#	%	#	%	#	%	#	%	#	%	#	%
Advanced	3	1	355	10	12,877	19	7	2	856	22	20,619	29
Proficient	82	19	1,123	30	30,208	43	29	7	819	21	19,286	28
Needs Improvement	183	43	1,399	37	18,584	27	176	41	1,175	31	19,913	28
Failing	155	37	865	23	7,935	11	213	50	987	26	10,313	15
Total Students	423		3,742		69,604		425		3,837		70,131	

MAKING SENSE OF TABLES

Panel A displays the percentages of tenth-grade students at Franklin High who fall into the four state-defined proficiency categories ("Advanced," "Proficient," "Needs Improvement," and "Failing"). These four categories and the total number of students define the rows in the panel. Across the top of the panel, columns first distinguish the subject specialty ("English Language Arts" and "Mathematics") and then academic year ("2002" through "2005"). By examining the entries in the fifth column, for example, you can see that only 1 percent of tenth-grade Franklin High students were assessed at the "Advanced" level in English language arts in 2005, whereas 37 percent were judged to be "Failing." By comparing the lists of percentages, column by column across the panel, you can examine how the proficiency distribution differed across cohorts of Franklin High tenth graders in 2002-05.

Panel B of Figure 1 presents similar information, but adds student frequencies (numbers of students) to the percentages shown in Panel A. Instead of the cross-cohort comparison in the first panel, however, Panel B provides a comparison between Franklin High students' proficiency distribution in 2005 and the performance distributions of tenth graders in the school district and the state for the same year. Notice that the "School" percentage of students at each proficiency level in Panel B is identical to the "2005" distributions in Panel A.

By reading this panel, Roger Bolton could see, for instance, that Franklin's tenth-grade students' mathematics proficiency was disappointing when compared to the district and state averages, because disproportionately more of Franklin's tenth graders fell into the "Failing" and "Needs Improvement" categories. However, it is difficult to select the proper columns and remember the numbers while trying to reach a conclusion about the educational significance of the differences. These difficulties suggest the value of capturing the key elements of the comparison in a graphical display.

Panel C of the table reorients the performance data to illustrate proficiency levels among various student groups. The proficiency categories are arrayed horizontally across the top of the table (within each of the two subject specialties), and student subgroups are labeled in rows down the left-hand side. These groupings—students' race/ethnicity, status, and qualification for free/reduced-price lunch—are critical reporting categories under No Child Left Behind legislation.

Panel C: Total Number of Students and Percentage at Each Proficiency Level, by Selected Student Background Characteristics, 2005 Academic Year

GRADE 10 % at Proficiency Level	ENGLISH LANGUAGE ARTS					MATHEMATICS				
	#	A	P	NI	F	#	A	P	NI	F
All Students	423	1	19	43	37	425	2	7	41	50
RACE/ETHNICITY										
African American/Black	201	1	16	40	43	201	1	4	35	60
Asian	38	0	15	75	10	37	9	31	50	10
Hispanic	116	2	10	47	41	119	0	3	43	54
Native American	2	n/a	n/a	n/a	n/a	2	n/a	n/a	n/a	n/a
White	59	0	55	19	26	58	6	7	48	39
Mixed/Other	7	n/a	n/a	n/a	n/a	8	n/a	n/a	n/a	n/a
STUDENT STATUS										
Regular	258	1	24	57	18	259	3	8	43	46
With Disabilities	85	0	19	30	51	85	1	6	39	54
English Language Learners	80	0	2	13	85	81	1	5	35	59
BY FREE/REDUCED-PRICE LUNCH (FRPL) STATUS										
Not Eligible for FRPL	110	2	27	39	32	110	5	10	49	36
Eligible for FRPL	313	1	16	44	39	315	1	6	38	55

As with Panel B, it is not easy to remember the numbers that are needed for any complex comparison among groups. There is simply too much information in the table for someone seeing it for the first time to grasp key patterns quickly. And, more importantly, there is so much information in the table that it could be used to address many different questions simultaneously.

THE VALUE OF GRAPHIC DISPLAYS

"Well, they say a picture's worth a thousand words," Roger Bolton said to his data team, "but I'm still stuck on what that picture is supposed to look like. There are so many types of graphs we could make. . . What would be best? How much detail do we want to provide?"

Roger recognizes that the most interesting and compelling themes in the state Comprehensive Assessment results are being obscured by its complicated, detailed, and generic tabular formatting. The challenge that he and his data team face is to find sensible ways to redisplay aggregate student assessment data so that the underlying educational stories and themes are transparent. Graphic displays are key tools for meeting this challenge.

The content, organization, labeling, and formatting of effective displays reflect the presenter's overall objectives for displaying the data and are tailored to the audience that will be examining the display. For instance, Roger may find it helpful to choose different ways of displaying the data when the audience is his faculty than when it is the district's central office staff. In our experience with schools, we have found that graphic displays geared toward stimulating discussions among school faculty can be less formal and more exploratory than those created for reports to the central office.

Once it has identified the broad objective and audience for a presentation, the data team should develop a list of specific educational questions to guide the creation of new graphic data displays. Many substantive questions can be informed by the student assessment results that are provided to schools. One effective way to present data and stimulate successful discussions among the faculty is to plan graphic displays that address a logical and interconnected sequence of these substantive questions. The underlying educational questions will determine the story that is communicated through the data presentation, which will differ from meeting to meeting and from school to school.

The underlying educational questions should also drive every aspect of the presentation of the assessment data and provide a rationale for why it is important to present the data one way rather than another. For example, the questions you are trying to answer should help you make the following decisions about your data presentation: Do you want to emphasize time trends? Are teachers and administrators interested in cohort comparisons? Is it important to analyze student performance by group? Do you want to focus the discussion on the students who fall into the lowest proficiencies or those who occupy the highest? Do you want to focus the audience's attention on the performance of your school's students relative to the average performance of students in the district or the state?

The educational questions your data team identifies provide the organizing themes the team should use to set the order and orientation of rows and columns in a table, or the order of bars and lines on a graph. These questions help you decide which features of the display to emphasize so that your audience will take note of them immediately. Your questions suggest how to orient the axes of a plot or the edges of the display so that important comparisons can be made. They determine the proper scales so that comparisons among the quantities displayed are informative and not misleading, and they suggest ways of wording the captions to focus the attention of the audience.

Remember that a good picture is worth a thousand words. Each compelling graph your data team creates from the statistics provided by the state will enable you to communicate a story to your audience. Good graphs can create a sense of urgency and stimulate conversations about possible explanations for the striking patterns they illustrate.

REORGANIZE YOUR ASSESSMENT DATA

Once the members of the Franklin High data team began to understand the importance of having educational questions drive the creation of graphs, they turned their attention to figuring out which questions to ask. "Let's just start with the basics," suggested data-team leader, Inés Romero. "Why don't we ask, 'How did our tenth graders perform in English language arts and mathematics last spring?'"

The team agreed that it will be able to focus faculty discussion by initially limiting attention to this simple question and to these two important subject areas. But they were not sure how to summarize the state-provided statistics so that everyone could immediately see the big picture and be able to participate in the discussion . . .

The data team's question—How did our students perform most recently in English language arts and mathematics?—can easily be addressed by displaying information from Panel A of Exhibit 3.1. To focus the faculty's attention on this question, Roger and his data team created a simple chart of the aggregate data. A variety of such charts can be readily plotted using a standard spreadsheet package, such as Microsoft Excel, once the aggregate data have been entered into the cells of a spreadsheet.

If Roger and his data team wanted to draw their audience's attention to the overall profile of tenth-grade student proficiencies in the subject areas of English language arts and mathematics separately, they could create two charts, one for each subject specialty. Exhibit 3.2 illustrates one method for doing this by using a vertical bar chart to display the Franklin High mathematics summary data. A similar chart could be used to display the English language arts performance.

Exhibit 3.2

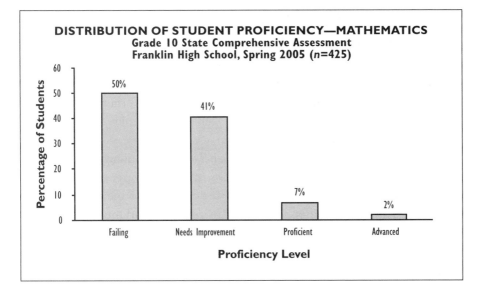

Notice that the data team has arrayed the proficiency categories along the horizontal axis of the chart, and the percentage of students within the school in each proficiency category is measured on a scale along the vertical axis. Each bar provides summary information for a different proficiency level of mathematics, with the height of the bar representing the percentage of students scoring at that level. The percentage of students scoring at each level has also been included above the corresponding bar to ease reading of the graph and to provide information the faculty may refer to in discussing the graph. Unlike the dense tabular representation of the mathematics data shown in Exhibit 3.1, vertical bar charts like this one naturally draw an audience's eyes toward a comparison of the percentage of students in each proficiency category.

There are many other kinds of charts that the data team could have chosen to display the performance distribution for Franklin High's students on the state math test. For example, horizontal bar charts and pie charts are also available in Excel and other spreadsheet software programs. The data team chose to use the vertical bar chart because it is one of the simplest, most easily understood data displays.

Notice that the data team has followed the standard practice of locating the conceptual "outcome" of the analysis (in this case, the percentage of the student body in each proficiency category) on the vertical axis and the conceptual "predictor" (here, the proficiency category itself) on the horizontal axis. It has also followed standard practice by arraying the "values" of the outcome and predictor along each axis so that they run from a conceptually low value to a conceptually high value. Thus, on the vertical axis, the student percentages run from "0%" at the bottom of the axis to "60%" at the top. On the horizontal axis, proficiency begins on the left with the "Failing" category and ends with "Advanced" on the right. In fact, in defining the horizontal axis of the vertical bar chart, the team had to reverse the order of the proficiency categories in the state-provided table (in Exhibit 3.1 the categories start with "Advanced" and end with "Failing").

The data team chose not to extend the metric of the vertical axis to include a "100%" value. Instead, it ended with the "60%" value because there were no data values that exceeded 60 percent. By limiting the range of values represented on the axis in this way, the team could "stretch out" the vertical bars and take advantage of the space available on the plot. The effect of such stretching is to magnify differences between the percentages of students in each category; modifying the scale of the vertical axis makes sense only if you think these differences are substantively important.

DRAW ATTENTION TO CRITICAL COMPARISONS

The data team decides to focus additional faculty discussion on the issue of math performance by asking, "How does our mathematics performance compare to the average performance of students in the state?" To address this question, the data team again creates a vertical bar chart based on summary statistics from Exhibit 3.1, but this time it superimposes the state proficiency percentages on the plot. To distinguish the school's performance from the state averages, the team uses a slightly different way of displaying the comparison data. The vertical bar chart for the state comparison is presented in Exhibit 3.3. Note that the mathematics proficiency profile for Franklin High tenth graders appears as it did in Exhibit 3.2. However, the team has superimposed a set of connected line segments to represent the average state performance across the four proficiencies. The team's use of the two strategies of display—vertical bars for Franklin High School, squares and line segments for the state—emphasizes the substantive differences in the two types of information the data team is presenting.

Exhibit 3.3

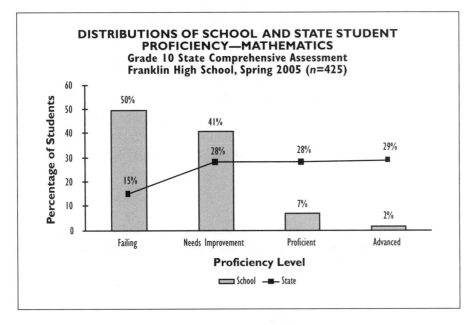

DISTRIBUTIONS OF SCHOOL AND STATE STUDENT
PROFICIENCY—MATHEMATICS
Grade 10 State Comprehensive Assessment
Franklin High School, Spring 2005 (*n*=425)

Understanding how students outside your school perform on the same assessment can provide benchmarks against which to compare the performance of your school's students. By contrasting the Franklin High School and the state average profiles, Roger and his data team hope to create a sense of urgency among their faculty colleagues. From the graph they produced, it will be clear that Franklin's 50 percent failure rate in tenth-grade mathematics is more than three times the state failure rate of 15 percent. The display also emphasizes immediately that the percentages of Franklin High students scoring in the "Advanced" and "Proficient" categories are far below the state's percentages. Roger hopes that drawing attention to these patterns will motivate his mathematics faculty to brainstorm possible explanations.

It is important to note that the data team should use caution in describing the percentage of Franklin High School's tenth graders who scored at the advanced level in mathematics, because the 2 percent figure represents only eight students. If the test were administered again, it is quite possible that the number of Franklin tenth graders scoring in the advanced range would change by three or four. This would change the percentage figure markedly. In other words, the 2 percent figure may be quite an imprecise estimate of the percentage of Franklin tenth graders with advanced math skills.

COMPARING THE PERFORMANCES OF GROUPS

There are a variety of ways to compare performance distributions for groups within an overall sample of students. These groups may be defined by any of the student demographic, status, or socioeconomic characteristics available in your database.

The two panels of Exhibit 3.4 display tenth-grade mathematics proficiencies disaggregated by student status. Although the two panels are based on the same information, they draw attention to different patterns. Exhibit 3.4a provides an informative extension of the vertical bar chart displayed in Exhibit 3.2 by adding a third dimension to the plot. This extra dimension breaks out the performances by proficiency level of three different groups: students in regular education programs, students with disabilities (SWDs), and English-language learners (ELLs).

Exhibit 3.4a

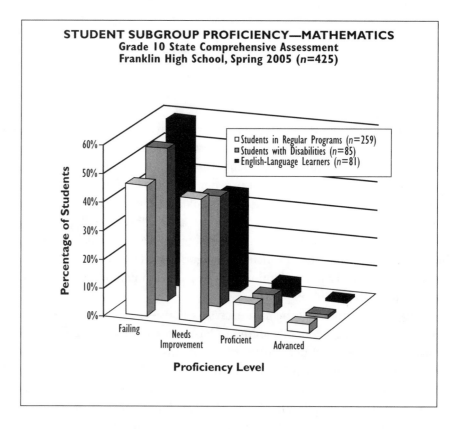

Exhibit 3.4b

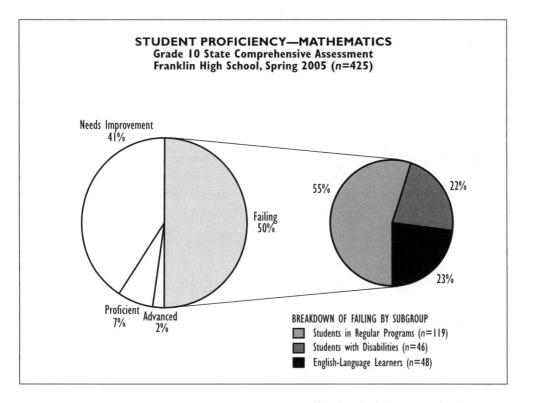

STUDENT PROFICIENCY—MATHEMATICS
Grade 10 State Comprehensive Assessment
Franklin High School, Spring 2005 (*n*=425)

Needs Improvement
41%

55%   22%

Failing
50%

23%

Proficient Advanced
7%   2%

BREAKDOWN OF FAILING BY SUBGROUP
Students in Regular Programs (*n*=119)
Students with Disabilities (*n*=46)
English-Language Learners (*n*=48)

In the new three-dimensional vertical bar chart, the faculty can now see how Franklin's tenth graders in each group perform across all proficiency levels. A faculty member who is interested in the performance of ELLs, for example, can examine the back row of bars and see that the highest percentage of these students scored at the "Failing" level. She can also quickly see that the failure rate for ELLs is higher than that for the other two groups.

The ever-present problems of measurement and sampling errors that come into play in any comparison are always exacerbated in group comparisons because the statistics that summarize average performance in each group can be based on very small numbers of students.

Despite these concerns, the three-dimensional vertical bar chart is particularly effective in drawing attention to differences in the shapes of the proficiency profiles across groups, making such differences evident to the faculty. This type of display also enables each audience member to see a complete set of information for every group at each level of performance. This enables teachers with differing instructional emphases—ELL or SWD, for example—to look at the same display and understand the performances of the specific groups they teach.

While Exhibit 3.4a is designed to draw the audience's attention to differences in the overall performance distribution of the three groups, Exhibit 3.4b is designed to break down different groups within a single proficiency level. The pie chart on the right side of Exhibit 3.4b shows the frequency of students, by group status, whose scores were in the "Failing" category. Notice that although Exhibit 3.4a showed that many SWDs and ELLs failed, Exhibit 3.4b shows that the majority of the failing students were actually in regular education programs. Pie charts and 3-D vertical bar charts are useful ways to disaggregate student performance to address questions about the differences among educationally important student groups. Based on the same original information, the Franklin High data team was able to prepare charts to fulfill different purposes—one that focused on overall performance and others that highlighted comparisons across groups.

DISPLAYING PERFORMANCE TRENDS

Principal Sandy Jenkins of Clark K-8 School was glad to see that her school had achieved adequate yearly progress (AYP), with more than 75 percent of the students meeting the target. She knew that the school's target would be substantially higher the following year. "As well it should be," Sandy thought to herself. There were a handful of schools in the area where nearly all of the students were performing in the proficient and advanced categories. Why shouldn't Clark be one of them? To get a conversation started with her faculty, Sandy asked the data team to produce some charts showing how student performance on the state test had changed over the last several years.

"When you say that you want us to display kids' average reading comprehension scores over time, what exactly do you mean?" asked Elvira Brown, a veteran teacher and member of the newly formed data team. "Are you asking us to create some pictures of how the third grade did this year, as compared to last year's third grade, and the one the year before, or are you asking us to follow the scores of the same group of kids over time, say from when they were in third grade until when they were in fifth grade?"

Exhibit 3.5 contains state-provided statistics summarizing the reading comprehension skills of students in the third through eighth grades at the Clark School. The figure lists the average reading comprehension score in each grade level for 2005 and for the previous two years. Fortunately, the state reading comprehension test had been vertically linked so that scores on the test can be compared across children of different ages, and from grade to grade. This vertical linking means that trends in average reading comprehension can be followed over time.

Exhibit 3.5

AVERAGE READING COMPREHENSION SCORES OF STUDENTS IN GRADES 3-8 AT CLARK K-8 SCHOOL		
ACADEMIC YEAR		
2003	2004	2005
Grade 3 249	250	245
Grade 4 253	252	255
Grade 5 259	257	256
Grade 6 260	261	259
Grade 7 258	263	264
Grade 8 264	262	265

To address their questions about differences and changes over time, the Clark data team used the data in Exhibit 3.5 to create two kinds of plots, each providing different insight into trends in the average reading comprehension of Clark students. Exhibit 3.6 contains a simultaneous vertical bar chart that displays overall differences in average reading comprehension by grade and by academic year. Exhibit 3.7 contains a trend-line plot that illustrates the average developmental trajectories of children in each cohort as they grew older.

Exhibit 3.6 displays the average reading scores in each grade within each academic year cohort. Each bar represents the average reading score (vertical axis) for students in a particular grade for that academic year, as recorded on the horizontal axis. The complete set of scores across the three years is represented by the three separate groups of vertical bars. Each bar is shaded slightly differently to distinguish between the various grades.

From this chart, the Clark data team can discern several interesting trends and idiosyncrasies in the reading comprehension data. First, notice that in any one academic year (a grouping of columns), children in the later grades are generally achieving higher reading comprehension scores than children in the earlier grades. A slight deviation from this trend occurred in 2003, however, when the average performance of the seventh grade fell below that of both the fifth and sixth grades, and in 2004, when this group (who were now eighth graders) also had relatively low scores. Sandy recognizes that there are many possible explanations for this pattern, such as weaknesses in the seventh-grade teaching team. However, she was relieved to see that the average performance of Clark's seventh-grade students in 2004 and 2005 was greater than the average performance of sixth-grade students in these years, and was higher than the average performance of the seventh-grade students in 2003. These were all comparisons Sandy could make quickly using the graph in Exhibit 3.6.

Exhibit 3.6

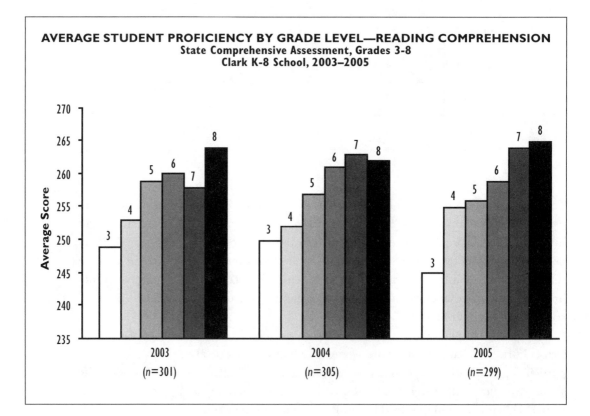

Another possible explanation for the relatively poor performance of Clark seventh graders in 2003 was that this cohort contained an unusually large group of children new to the school who had not had the benefit of the solid teaching at Clark in the early grades. An important follow-up question for Sandy is whether the group of Clark seventh graders in 2003 made real progress over the next year—their last in the school. Exhibit 3.7 provides an alternative display of the information in Exhibit 3.5, with an orientation that helps Sandy answer her question.

Exhibit 3.7

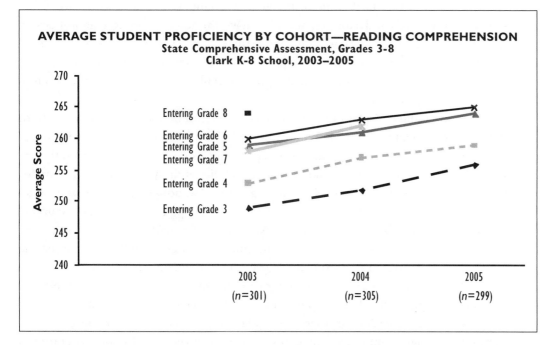

The display in Exhibit 3.7 recognizes that the group of children who entered seventh grade in the 2003 academic year become the eighth-grade group in the 2004 academic year. Of course, it may be that not all the children are the same; some may have left the school and new children may have entered. However, providing that the data team is prepared to assume that most of the children who started out in the seventh grade in 2003 did indeed go on to eighth grade at the Clark School the next year, it can attach a developmental interpretation to the average trajectories in Exhibit 3.7.

Each line in Exhibit 3.7 plots the average achievement trajectory for a group of children over time. The label beside each line indicates the grade that group was in during the 2003 school year. Notice, due to limitations in the dataset itself, that there are only two data points for the children who were in the seventh grade in 2003, and only one data point for the children who were in the eighth grade in 2003.

A quick look at Exhibit 3.7 shows that the group of seventh graders in 2003 improved its average reading performance markedly during the next school year, alleviating somewhat the concern about the academic performance of this group.

While the graphs in Exhibits 3.6 and 3.7 are based on the same data, the emphases are different. If there is little student mobility in and out of Clark, Exhibit 3.7 illustrates the longitudinal progress of the "same" group of children over time. Note that children entering Clark in the third grade in the 2003 academic year, whose scores are represented by the lowest trajectory on the plot, have the lowest reading comprehension scores of any group in the dataset. Of course, this is to be expected, since in any school year they are the youngest children represented. Also notice that the average rate of growth over the three-year period for this group essentially mirrors that of the children in the other entering grades.

The longitudinal display of the reading comprehension scores highlights a pattern that is more difficult to discern in Exhibit 3.6. In Exhibit 3.7, the entire average developmental trajectory of the third graders who entered in 2003 lies entirely beneath the trajectory for the entering fourth graders, which itself lies entirely below the trajectory for entering fifth graders, and so on. The ranking of the elevations of these several trajectories by entering grade makes sense, given the expected dependence of reading comprehension on children's grade and age. An exception to this pattern, noted above, is the relatively low performance of the group entering seventh grade in 2003. However, the graph shows the progress this group made over the subsequent school year.

In deciding which display to present at the upcoming faculty meeting, the Clark data team recognizes that Exhibits 3.6 and 3.7, while based on identical information, are designed for very different purposes. If the data team wants to emphasize the pattern of third-through-eighth-grade average scores from cohort to cohort of students in order to draw attention to noticeable—and substantial—deviations from expected patterns, the simultaneous vertical bar chart in Exhibit 3.6 is preferable. This chart draws attention to the low average performance of the 2003 seventh graders relative to students in other grades in the same year and to the seventh-grade groups in the subsequent two school years. However, if the data team wants to focus attention on how the skills of a group of students develop over time, the connected line segments in Exhibit 3.7 present this information clearly and simply.

In labeling and explaining graphs showing student performance in different school years, it is important to be clear about whether the display illustrates trends in achievement for the same group of students over time, or whether it illustrates cohort-to-cohort differences over a number of years in the performance of students at the same grade level. Exhibits like 3.6 that display only cohort-to-cohort differences are not helpful in tracking true progress or "growth" over time. Exhibits like 3.7 do display progress over time if there is little or no student mobility. Chapter 9, which discusses the district role in supporting data work in schools, explains how a good student tracking system is invaluable in supporting the work of school-based data teams. For example, a good data-tracking system would allow a data team to construct a graph showing the progress of students who had been at Clark for at least three years—long enough to benefit from high-quality instruction.

COMPONENTS OF GOOD DISPLAYS

With the endless possibilities available in computer software programs, it is easy to become enamored of extremely fancy, complicated graphs. However, the main goal of any plot or graph is to convey complicated information in a simple, clear manner so that questions of educational significance can be understood, debated, and resolved. The following are suggestions for creating good data displays that school teams we have worked with have found useful:

* Make an explicit and informative title for every figure in which you indicate critical elements of the chart, such as who was assessed, the number of students whose performance is summarized in the figure, what subject specialty, and when.

* Make clear labels for each axis in a plot, or each row and column in a table.

* Make sensible use of the space available on the page, with the dimensions, axes, and themes that are most important for the educational discussion being the most dominant in the display.

* Keep plots uncluttered and free of unnecessary detail, extraneous features, and gratuitous cross-hatching and patterns.

* When labeling and explaining graphs showing student performance in different school years, be clear about whether the display illustrates trends in achievement for the same group of students over time, as in Exhibit 3.7, or whether it is illustrating differences in performance from one cohort of students to another at the same grade level over a period of years, as in Exhibit 3.6.

Exhibit 3.8

TIPS FOR CREATING EFFECTIVE DATA DISPLAYS	
PROVIDE COMPLETE TITLE	**MAKE CHART SIMPLE AND EASY TO READ**
• Assessment name and subject • Grade-level tested • School name • Date of assessment • Number of students tested	• Appropriate choice of chart style • Good use of space and color • Fonts large enough to read easily • Clearly labeled legend and axes • Appropriate y-axis scale • Data-point values, where helpful

LEADING EFFECTIVE DISCUSSIONS

Roger Bolton was aware that several teachers were not looking forward to Franklin High's first faculty meeting of the year, which they knew would be devoted entirely to talking about results of the state math exam. He could imagine that they expected two hours of listening to him drone on about student performance in a subject that most of them didn't teach. Moreover, he anticipated that teachers' anxiety about math would prevent many of them from engaging fully in the discussion he hoped to have.

To maximize the effectiveness and power of your data team's clear and compelling charts, school leaders must use them to stimulate a conversation among your faculty members, specifically about what they see in the data, what questions the data raise, and how they could go about finding answers to these new questions. School leaders we have worked with who successfully involve teachers in addressing learning problems suggest that it is not enough to put copies of charts of state assessment results in faculty mailboxes or to give a lecture about what the charts show. Instead, they actively involve teachers in the data by giving them an opportunity to make sense of the data for themselves, encouraging them to ask questions, and offering them a chance to experience and discuss the actual questions on the test.

PROVIDE OPPORTUNITIES FOR TEACHERS TO WORK WITH THE DATA

Once the data team prepares effective displays, the information displayed in the charts will seem clear to team members. One approach to presenting the data is to ask a team member to present the various charts to your faculty while pointing out the highlights and conclusions for each graph. However, most teachers recognize that the best way to encourage learning among their students is to give them an opportunity for hands-on exploration, and the same holds true when school leaders "teach" faculty to learn from data. If teachers puzzle over the data displays for themselves, they are likely to learn much more from them, and this process will also build their confidence in and comfort with analyzing data.

One particularly effective way of engaging teachers in data analysis is to distribute a few displays and to ask teachers to "pair share" with the person next to them about what they see. This approach involves everyone in talking right away—in just seconds the room will be alive with discussion. The charts ensure that these conversations will be highly focused around the questions your data team has addressed. Because this exercise allows teachers to formulate their ideas with a partner before being asked to speak in front of the whole group, we find that participants are better prepared to join in a large group discussion and share their observations.

ENCOURAGE TEACHERS TO ASK QUESTIONS

Wanting to capitalize on the group energy that the pair shares generated, Franklin principal Roger Bolton asked the faculty to huddle into ten groups throughout the library. History teacher Pamela Eddy, who was initially reluctant to become involved in any discussion of data—especially math data—found herself surprisingly interested in continuing to explore math performance at Franklin High School. In her group of eight, Pamela volunteered to be the note taker, recording the group's progress on the next step of data exploration: brainstorming questions.

Attitudes toward data vary widely in schools. There are plenty of "data skeptics" who believe either that student assessment data cannot tell them anything they do not already know or insist that such data can be manipulated to support whatever story the teller wishes. Typically, there are also some "data advocates" who believe that student assessment results contain the answers to solving student learning problems and that finding these answers is just a matter of becoming better at data analysis. In reality, student assessment data is neither this weak nor this powerful. The real value in looking at this kind of data is not that it provides answers, but that it inspires questions.

To maximize the potential of data to help generate questions, school leaders we have worked with have found it extremely helpful to use a structured protocol. One particularly engaging and productive protocol is the Question Formulation Technique, which is described in detail under Selected Protocols at the end of this book. The basic premise of this technique is that in order for people to take ownership of an issue, they need to participate actively in defining it. The protocol involves asking small groups to brainstorm questions about a particular issue. As questions are offered, a note taker records them, exactly as stated, for the group to see. After a certain point, the facilitator asks the group to identify the most important question. The group then brainstorms a new set of questions about the priority question. From this new set of questions, a "final" priority question is chosen. We have found that this process enables educators to focus deeply on an important issue, encourages them to listen to all voices, and provides a useful brake on the usual impulse to jump to solutions.

Once teams have brainstormed a list of the questions that the data overview inspired, you can engage your entire faculty in a discussion of what data are necessary to begin answering the priority question. At some schools, the data team functions as a resource for collecting this information. For example, at a large group meeting, Franklin High faculty members may determine that in order to make progress on helping students become better writers, they need to know what classes struggling writers take, whether students who perform poorly on state writing tests also perform poorly in the classroom, and if there are opportunities to adapt the new writing curriculum to students' specific needs. Once the faculty has identified the information it needs, the data team can pursue it and report back with new evidence. When faculty are committed to exploring many data sources before acting, data skeptics and data advocates alike may modify their opinions about the role of student assessment results in helping solve problems in student learning.

ALLOW TEACHERS TO EXPERIENCE AND DISCUSS THE ACTUAL TEST

After looking at a data overview—or before, which can work equally well—you may want to let your faculty experience actual test questions from the relevant assessment. If your state releases actual or sample test questions, you can share them with your teachers. We have worked with several schools that require all teachers in the building to take the same state assessments as their students, either in full or in part, and occasionally under the exam conditions and administration guidelines that are in place for students. By actually experiencing the test themselves, teachers learn firsthand about the content that is being assessed, the ways it is assessed, and the stamina and mindset that may be needed to perform well.

The most significant benefit to having teachers take the test, however, may be in giving them an opportunity to discuss what they learned from the experience. We have found the Continuum Protocol to be an excellent way to allow a group of people to share their reactions to the test-taking experience.[1] This protocol involves asking individuals to stand up and place themselves along a horseshoe-shaped continuum, with each end of the horseshoe representing the extremes of an opinion. For the purposes of a discussion about a test-taking experience, the extremes at each end of the horseshoe could be, "This test does accurately measure what I think our students should know and be able to do" and "This test does not accurately measure what I think our students should know and be able to do." People who find themselves somewhere between the two extremes can place themselves in the location that best represents their view. One advantage of this protocol is that it allows everyone in the room to state their opinion, which they do by simply choosing where to stand. The facilitator can then ask individuals at various locations along the continuum to explain why they placed themselves where they did. After a number of teachers have spoken, the facilitator asks if, given what they have heard, anyone would like to change his or her position and then, if appropriate, encourages an open discussion of the issues raised to that point.

Many educators we have worked with find that this protocol offers a safe way to initiate a candid discussion about attitudes around testing. Teachers hold a wide range of opinions about the value of assessments and the consequences of holding all children to high standards. Acknowledging that these tensions exist among your faculty members and allowing people to have a structured conversation about them can be an important step in helping people work together to address the issues raised in your data overview.

4

DIGGING INTO DATA

Ethan Mintz, Sarah E. Fiarman, and Tom Buffett

AT A FRANKLIN HIGH SCHOOL MATH DEPARTMENT MEETING, principal Roger Bolton shared a graph (see Exhibit 4.1) that the data team had made of the previous year's state test results. "At the last faculty meeting, you wondered whether there were particular content areas where students need to improve. Based on the data from the state test, what do you think?"

"I'd say all of them," replied Adelina. Eddie, a veteran geometry teacher, jumped in, "It's very clear from looking at this graph that our students are just not prepared to do math when they get to high school. We're teaching the curriculum, but they're not getting it. Look, they're having trouble with number sense and measurement—they should know those by the time they get to high school! We need to go back to the fundamentals and get them ready for high school math."

With test scores in hand, Eddie is ready to address Franklin students' low math performance. He thinks he knows the problem—students' lack of "basic skills"—and he has a solution: drill those basics. The question for Eddie and other educators at this point in the improvement cycle is, "Do you really know what problem you are trying to solve?"

Before committing to a particular course of action or investing time in developing possible solutions, it is important that you fully understand the learner-centered problem, which we define as a problem of understanding or skill that underlies students' performance on assessments. "Learner-centered problem" means that the problem is about learning, not that learners are the problem. We know that, in reality, no school faces just one learner-centered problem. The goal of this chapter is to help schools identify a learner-centered problem that is common to many students and that, if solved, would help meet your larger goals for students. Educators tend to skip this step, jumping right to developing an action plan and a solution to the problem of low performance. Those educators often find themselves back in the same place the following year, with no improvement to show for their work.

Without an investigation of the data, schools risk misdiagnosing the problem. Poor test scores in geometry and measurement could be a result of weak fundamentals, but they could also be the result of inadequate amounts of homework and independent practice on the topic, students' lack of experience with real-world applications of the topic, the fact that the content is taught long before the test and students aren't retaining what they've learned, or that the content is taught too late for students to use their knowledge on the current year's standardized assessment. Each of these problems requires a different solution; digging into your data helps ensure a more accurate diagnosis of the problem.

Exhibit 4.1

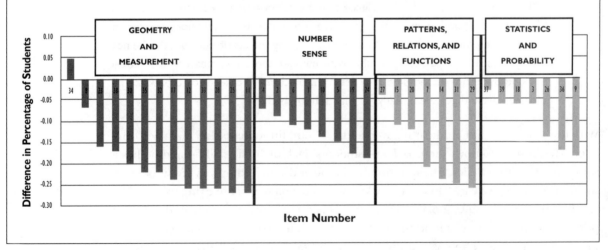

PERCENTAGE OF STUDENTS ANSWERING EACH MULTIPLE-CHOICE ITEM CORRECTLY
Grade 10 State Comprehensive Assessment—Mathematics
Franklin High School, Spring 2005 (*n*=425)

Standardized test data, which many principals and teachers are under considerable pressure to use for improvement planning, can be a good starting point for your conversation, but they rarely provide all you need to know to improve achievement at your school. Aggregate data displays don't tell you why students performed the way that they did, and they don't tell you anything about the performance of individual students. Schools have a wide variety of data they can draw on, including test scores, class projects, homework, performances, lab reports, reading journals, teacher observations, and student focus groups. The data inventory you completed in chapter 1 is a good resource for identifying the data available in your school.

The process of using data to identify the learner-centered problem is an iterative, inquiry-based process. The questions raised by your data overview should lead to further investigation of the data, which inevitably leads to new questions and investigations. Recognizing both the messiness and the richness of this process, this chapter shows how to use data wisely so that you identify the learner-centered problem and avoid the "analysis paralysis" that can come from aimless, endless data analysis.

There are two main steps when using data to identify the learner-centered problem in your school: looking carefully at a single data source and digging into other data sources.

LOOK CAREFULLY AT A SINGLE DATA SOURCE

At the Clark School, the leadership team was trying to figure out what to do next with the faculty. "We generated lots of interesting questions about reading at the last meeting," said principal Sandy Jenkins. "Now we need to figure out how we're going to answer them."

"Well, I think we've milked the state test for all it offers, which is not much," said Vivian Muteba, a fourth-grade teacher. "It's really frustrating that we lose so many days to students taking the tests, and then the tests only tell us that students are a '3' in reading, or have a scale score of 252—what does that mean, anyway?"

"Besides that, we're doing pretty well on the state test, and I don't think a lot of teachers here think the state test reflects all that they're trying to do with kids," said Frank DeLeon, a sixth-grade teacher. "I don't think teachers really want to spend any more time looking at the test."

The first step in digging into data to identify a learner-centered problem is to look carefully at a single data source. This step begins with choosing a data source based on your data overview and your context. Examining the information from that data source can deepen faculty members' understanding of student thinking and challenge their assumptions about students, which in turn can lead them to hone their definition of the learner-centered problem and to generate new questions. The process of digging into a single data source provides both momentum and direction for further investigation by creating a sense of urgency and curiosity. It can also encourage teachers to refine their initial hunches about the learner-centered problem.

CHOOSING A SINGLE DATA SOURCE AS A STARTING PLACE

For many schools, the decision about where to begin data analysis amid the mountains of data available in the school can seem overwhelming. While the data overview generated in chapter 3 provides a good place to begin, the dilemma quickly resurfaces with the questions, concerns, and puzzles that emerge from analysis of the data overview. What next? In our experience, schools too often stay on the surface level of data analysis. Pressed to solve significant problems quickly, many educators take the swift route: look at a table or two, make a judgment based on what they already think is true, and decide to address a problem that they can solve easily and that doesn't require much change on their part. This rapid response often leads to a "stuck point," where schools find themselves either repeating the same pattern by continuing to teach what they've always taught and getting the same results, or by throwing up their hands in frustration and blaming the students for not learning what they are teaching. Teachers may feel that their efforts in the classroom are not reflected in student performance on the "tests that count," and that they are facing the same challenges over and over again. Or, in schools where there is little external pressure to improve what seems to be adequate performance, there may be a different sort of stuck point, where teachers feel that there is not much need for improvement.

Digging into a single data source can help a school move past stuck points like these. Focusing initially on a single data source slows down the common tendency to leap to solutions, makes the data analysis process manageable, and provides an opportunity to move beyond generalizations about the learner-centered problem. Which data source you choose as a starting point will depend on your questions and your context.

The first thing to consider is, What questions do you have about the student learning problem, and what data will help answer those questions? While many schools choose to continue to examine the state assessments that provided the initial basis for their inquiry in the data overview, this choice depends in part on what information is available in the state assessments. In states where the assessments include performance by content strand or standards as well as by individual items, schools often can mine the assessments for information that illuminates the learner-centered problem. In states where there is little to no information on content strands, standards, or individual items, schools must turn to another data source to continue their inquiry into the problem.

The next consideration is context: What data will be most compelling for the faculty? At a school like Franklin High that has been designated by the state as needing improvement because of its poor state assessment results, the faculty often feels a lot of pressure to raise performance on the state test. We have seen many school leaders use the pressure of external accountability as a catalyst for improvement. Teachers are willing to dig more deeply into the state test because they and their students are being judged by the results. At a school like Clark that doesn't face this external pressure, school leaders may choose different data, such as day-to-day student work or writing portfolios, to establish both the need and desire for improvement.

UNDERSTANDING STUDENT THINKING

At Franklin, the math department continued to look at the state test results. Department head Mallory Golden broke the teachers into groups based on content-area expertise to look at particular strands and to see if there were any specific skills or understandings that led to students answering those particular questions incorrectly. The algebra group reported that students had the most difficulty with multi-step problems containing variables and equations containing fractions. The geometry group said that students were particularly challenged by anything three-dimensional or requiring proofs, while the statistics/probability group cited student difficulties with interpreting data.

The faculty looked at items from the test in each of those areas. "Do we see any patterns across the different content areas?" asked Mallory Golden.

"I wonder if the problem is language," said Adelina. "Many of these problems require a lot of reading. Maybe kids don't read well, or don't want to read to do math. They seem to do better on problems where they just do math and don't have to read so much."

"I still think the problem is basic skills," said Eddie. "A lot of these problems have a bunch of steps, and if you make a mistake early on, you'll get the problem wrong."

"On the language front, it seems like there's a lot of math vocabulary. I know I taught my students this statistics material, but I didn't call it 'statistics,' and they don't seem to have recognized what they were supposed to do on the test," said Jean.

Mallory felt that they had moved far beyond thinking that "math" was the problem at Franklin, but she knew they still needed a better understanding of the problem before they could do anything about it.

A student's response on an assessment is just the end product of his or her thinking. In analyzing data to identify a student learning problem, it is critical to look not just at the end product of the work, but at the path a student took to get there. Understanding how students arrived at a wrong answer or a poor result is important in knowing how to help them learn to get to the right answer or a good result. Investigating students' thinking processes helps answer questions such as, Do students have any skills and knowledge to build on, or do they need a total reteaching of a particular content area? Are students lacking skills and content knowledge, or is the design of the assessment itself giving them difficulty? Working to find answers to these questions will help you identify a meaningful learner-centered problem that affects student performance.

We have seen many schools use item analysis of tests (both state tests and school-based content tests) to understand student thinking. In item analysis, you first look at test items (i.e., questions) in groups by content (such as statistics and probability) or type (such as multiple-choice, short-answer, essay) to see if there were any specific skills or areas of understanding that might have led students to answer the question incorrectly. Then you look for patterns across item groups on the tests. Finally, you look more closely at individual test items to hypothesize why students responded to certain questions in particular ways.

When striving to detect patterns and understand student thinking, it's important for teachers to recognize that students, unless they are guessing wildly at answers, have some logic in how they go about answering questions and doing their work, even if that logic leads them to wrong answers or low-quality work. The teacher's work, in looking closely at the available data, is to try to find that logic pattern. A teacher who understands how a student thinks and approaches schoolwork will have a clearer sense of what the student needs as a learner. She will also be able to provide instruction that builds on what the student knows and addresses what the student doesn't know. At some schools, teachers take the state assessment themselves, keeping track of their own thinking along the way, so they can begin to understand how students think when they take the assessment.

One of the tensions in using data to improve learning and teaching is the need to figure out the balance between two goals, both of which demand the scarce resource of time. The first goal is having teachers participate in the data analysis process so that they feel ownership of the learner-centered problem, and so that the data analysis is something they do instead of something that is done to them. In other words, teachers are more likely to see the learner-centered problem as a problem that they want to do something about if they've had a major role in identifying it. The second goal, however, is to get to the deeper level of analysis that will help identify the problem. At some schools, data teams or instructional leadership teams do the initial stages of the analysis in order to save time for teachers to focus on the deeper analysis. After a smaller team has done some preliminary analysis (including, but not necessarily limited to, the data overview described in chapter 3), these schools then involve the faculty in a more in-depth analysis to identify the learner-centered problem.

For instance, at one school we know, the data manager makes a chart with each student in a particular grade displayed in a row. Across the top of the chart, he puts each item on the state test. He then highlights each student who scored below proficient, and each item on which fewer than 80 percent of students answered correctly. Before he enlarges the charts to poster size, he blacks out students' names in order to promote collective responsibility and prevent teachers from dismissing the results of particular students. He does this for each subject and each grade that takes the state test. The colorful, highlighted posters become a jumping-off point for discussions with grade-level teams and the whole faculty about the nature of the learner-centered problem. At another school, data-team members show teachers one or two items from the state test or one piece of student writing, and then ask them what they notice about those items and why students may have responded in the ways they did. While they would never draw broad conclusions from any single test item, many school leaders find that getting to the level of a single item or a single student's performance engages teachers and gets them talking about students' thinking and learning in a way that is grounded in evidence.

CHALLENGING ASSUMPTIONS

At Clark, the instructional leadership team thought that reading journals might provide insight into how students think about and respond to what they read. The team took a random sample of ten third-grade students. After examining and discussing the journals, they chose one representative journal to bring to the faculty.

At the faculty meeting, teachers described what they noticed in the student's journal while another teacher put their comments up on chart paper: "The student articulated the plot of the story he read"; "He described each character in detail"; "He described plot details sequentially, even though the story started in the middle of the action"; "He started each paragraph with a thesis statement."

A seventh-grade teacher commented, "I think we're missing important information about this child's skills as a reader—he's good at listing everything and pointing out factual information, but what about reading and thinking between the lines?"

"That's a really sophisticated skill." Kristina, a third-grade teacher, jumped in, saying, "You all work on that in the upper grades. Our job is to make sure they know what's happening in the book—and that's plenty hard as it is! Plus, it's hard for kids to decode and read between the lines at the same time."

"I disagree," Lynne, a second-grade teacher, said. "Reading comprehension is much more than factual recall."

Examining student work helps to surface and challenge many assumptions—assumptions about what students can and cannot do, about which students can do what, and about why students are or are not able to do something. Challenging these assumptions is critical for three reasons. First, you want the clearest understanding possible about the student learning problem, and assumptions often obscure this understanding by taking the place of evidence. Second, teachers fundamentally have to believe that students are capable of something different from the results in the current data. Otherwise, why bother putting any effort into helping students learn? And third, the solutions for the problem will require changes in what faculty members do on a day-to-day basis. Making significant changes in what you do often requires changing what you believe. Opportunities for teachers to share their interpretations of student data provide occasions to address these fundamental beliefs about learning and teaching.

Starting with data and grounding the conversation in evidence from the data keeps the discussion focused on what we see rather than what we believe. In the Clark example above, the teachers started by noting what they observed in the student's reading journal before they made any judgments of how "good" the work was or what sort of reader the student was. The seventh-grade teacher drew on evidence from the journal to pose her question about "reading between the lines." The third-grade teacher's response, which was not grounded in the student's journal, surfaced an important assumption—that reading between the lines was too sophisticated for third graders.

Data can also be used to challenge assumptions. At one high school, the principal started a fall faculty meeting by presenting several graphs to his faculty (see Exhibit 4.2). He told the faculty that the percentages represented groups of students but didn't say what groups they were. After giving teachers some time to think about who the numbers might represent, the principal told them group one was girls and group two was boys. The first-quarter honor roll was 83 percent girls, while the group of students receiving two or more Fs in the first quarter was 82 percent boys. The data surprised the faculty, who had assumed the poor scores were from other student groups, like students with disabilities or students who qualified for free/reduced-price lunch. The data, and teachers' surprise, led to discussion and exploration of why boys were having less academic success than girls.

It is not uncommon to make assumptions about which students are "low performers" or "high performers." Taking a closer look at student work can often challenge these assumptions, and in so doing, strengthen understanding of what students do and do not know how to do. In one middle school, teachers were analyzing data from a short reading-comprehension assessment for seventh graders. When they began to look closely at student work, a special education teacher pointed to the work of one of her students, Delmar, who got four of the five questions correct, including the short-answer questions, putting him among the best of the seventh graders during this particular assessment. The teachers were stunned. This was a completely unexpected result from Delmar, who had a very difficult time staying focused in class. As teachers talked about Delmar's responses and his work on the assessment, one of the teachers said, "This makes things confusing." This was "confusing" in a good way—the picture of Delmar had changed from one of a student who "spaces out" in class and has little academic strength to a student who merits a closer look and higher teacher expectations. This new, "confusing" picture of Delmar pushed the teachers to look more closely at all of their students' work to find the places where their students showed particular strengths. It also reminded them not to make easy, false assumptions about students' skills and capabilities.

Exhibit 4.2

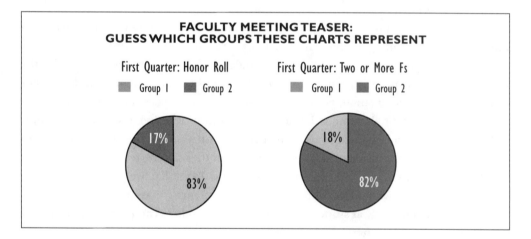

FACULTY MEETING TEASER:
GUESS WHICH GROUPS THESE CHARTS REPRESENT

First Quarter: Honor Roll   First Quarter: Two or More Fs

Group 1   Group 2   Group 1   Group 2

17%   18%

83%   82%

DIG INTO OTHER DATA SOURCES

At Clark, the faculty meeting about the third-grade student's reading journal continued.

"I think that reading has to be more than a mechanical process at all grade levels," said a second-grade teacher. "All students need to think about what they read and make inferences from the text. Listing facts is important, but it's only part of what reading is all about."

"I agree with you," said Jae. "But I'm wondering if we're making too big a deal about this—after all, we're only looking at one student's journal. How do we know that this is an issue for more than this student?"

After analyzing a single data source in depth, you will have learned some things to help identify the learner-centered problem on which you will focus your improvement efforts. Undoubtedly, though, the process has raised more questions than can be answered with a single data source. All data sources are limited in the information they provide. Any single test or classroom assignment addresses only a portion of what you want children to learn. No single data source can provide a full picture of students' abilities.

If you rely on one data source to identify a problem, it is unlikely that you will select a problem that is worthy of your ongoing time and attention—in part because you may be identifying a problem with the data source rather than a problem you can address as a faculty. Just as you might ask your friends and check consumer reports online before buying a new car, examining multiple data sources will raise your confidence that you will select the right problem to tackle. Furthermore, digging into other sources will help make sure your faculty shares expectations for what students should know and be able to do in a variety of contexts.

We know many schools that look closely at multiple data sources with the purpose of understanding student thinking. These data can include students' projects, classwork, or homework. The process of "looking at student work" (sometimes known by the acronym LASW) can give teachers considerable insight into students' thinking.[1] For example, by examining students' homework on questions that deal with statistics, the math teachers at Franklin might be able to determine whether the students simply didn't grasp the term "statistics," as Jean surmised, or whether they were faltering in their understanding of key statistical concepts. At another school, teachers bring two or three student essay samples to LASW meetings, where they collectively look for evidence of students' ability to write topic sentences, provide evidence for assertions, and so forth. By looking collaboratively at students' everyday work, teachers can deepen their understanding of students' strengths and misconceptions.

TRIANGULATING DATA SOURCES

By "triangulating" your findings from multiple data sources—that is, by analyzing other data to illuminate, confirm, or dispute what you learned through your initial analysis—you will be able to identify your problem with more accuracy and specificity. When triangulating sources, it can be helpful to draw on different types of assessments (such as tests, portfolios, and student conferences) and on assessments taken at different intervals (such as daily, at the end of a curriculum unit, and at the end of a grading period or semester), and to look for both patterns and inconsistencies across student responses to the assessments. Schools that look at state data as their initial data source might next examine classroom tests and homework. Schools that focus initially on daily classroom work might consult annual or quarterly assessments.

At Clark, the discussion of reading journals brought the issue of reading between the lines to the surface. Could it be that the prompts to which students responded in the reading journal encouraged factual responses? Could it be something about the process of writing that interfered with students' ability to show how well they could read? Clark teachers will need to examine other data sources to investigate whether students are able to read between the lines in other contexts.

A rich source of data is the students themselves. For example, after doing an analysis of the wrong answers students gave on the state test, teachers at one middle school were intrigued by the common mistakes students made. They decided to conduct focus groups with students to understand why they seemed to be making the same types of mistakes. Students are an important and underused source of insight into their own thinking, and having focus groups with students to talk about their thinking can have a positive impact on your efforts to identify a problem underlying low student performance.

When triangulating data, be prepared to be surprised. It is important to approach the process of digging deeper into other data sources with the idea that you will find something new. When the goal is merely to confirm a hypothesis or assumption, only particular pieces of data tend to be looked at, and the work often stops when the original belief is confirmed. Instead, look for and embrace unexpected trends and leads. School leaders can play an important role by modeling the ideas that it is acceptable to ask questions and that faculty should expect to understand something new about student learning by the end of a meeting. In this context, it's important that school leaders not try to portray themselves as all-knowing experts. Schools should be led by what they discover, which will lead to new questions to investigate as they identify the learner-centered problem.

At Franklin, for example, the math teachers examined unit tests and homework and realized that students correctly answered basic-skills problems when all they had to do was use a single skill. This finding debunked Eddie's assertion that the issue was basic skills and led teachers back to the state test, where they noticed that there were few problems that required only a single skill, and those few problems had words that placed the skill in some sort of real-world context instead of just presenting the problem in numbers and asking students to solve it. When they examined classwork to see if there were differences among students, they were surprised to see that many students with disabilities were solving complex problems more accurately than regular education students. This finding did not match the state test results, where students with disabilities performed worse than regular education students on all problems, including complex problems. When teachers investigated further by talking with students and teachers and looking at the classwork again, they realized that students with disabilities were approaching their classwork differently. With the support of the special education teachers, students were highlighting important words in the problem and breaking the problem into separate pieces. Teachers saw some evidence of students using this approach on unit tests, but the students said they forgot the approach when it came to the state test. After examining multiple data sources, sometimes returning to data sources with new questions, Franklin is closer to identifying a learner-centered problem as having something to do with complex math problems, which few students seem to have a process for solving, or a process they can apply in different contexts.

DEVELOPING A SHARED UNDERSTANDING OF THE KNOWLEDGE AND SKILLS STUDENTS NEED

At the Clark School, the instructional leadership team decided to take a "slice" of student work to investigate what students were doing with reading and what "reading between the lines" looked like in different grade levels and content areas.[2]

The slice was of all the classwork and homework that 30 students, chosen randomly from the first, fifth, and eighth grades, had completed from noon one day until noon the next day. The faculty used one of their afternoons together on an early release day to examine the work and discuss it.

"What did you notice about the work students are doing in reading?" asked principal Sandy Jenkins.

"I noticed that students use art to show meaning. The first graders drew pictures to go with the stories they wrote, and the eighth graders made storyboards interpreting scenes from the book they're reading."

"I noticed that there was evidence that fifth-grade students had read at home for homework—the reading log signed by their parents—but I wasn't sure if students had discussed their reading at home or at school, or had written anything down, or in some way showed their thinking about what they had read."

"I noticed that a lot of the reading students seemed to be doing was pretty factual, so there wasn't much cause to read between the lines. At least in the work we saw, the reading that students were responding to tended to be short, informative pieces, like a section of a history book or science book that students were answering questions about."

"It seems like students are pretty much giving us what we ask for—maybe we're not asking for enough."

While you refine your definition of the learner-centered problem, you also build a common understanding among teachers of the knowledge and skills students need to have—in other words, what you expect students to know and be able to do, and how well they are meeting your expectations. Perhaps you want students to be "proficient" or "advanced" or "good readers" or "complex problem-solvers," but what do those words really mean? Do you all agree on what you expect, and at what point do you think it's a problem if students aren't meeting those expectations? As teachers examine various data sources, they develop a richer understanding of the curriculum and external standards, as well as shared internal standards for high-quality work.

The process of examining and discussing student data can feel threatening to teachers, especially if there is not a norm of collaborative practice at a school. Historically, teachers have taught in isolation, in the privacy of their classrooms, and rarely have shared their practice in any concrete form. It is therefore not surprising that teachers often feel exposed when they share the work of their students with peers. Teachers need to know that they are not opening themselves up to a free-wheeling critique based on their peers' perceptions of their practice. Structuring conversations using protocols assures teachers that they will have the opportunity to be heard and that peers' comments will not be speculative, but will be grounded in the student work in front of them and moderated by a facilitator.

At the same time, teachers need to feel comfortable asking challenging, constructive questions of each other. Collaboratively examining student work often leads to important new insights. Having a built-in expectation and a designated time to ask probing questions supports the constructive practice of talking specifically about student learning. Finally, by agreeing to certain ground rules for examining student work and by using relevant protocols, you can ensure that the conversation includes multiple voices rather than just the usual ones. This leads to greater consistency in defining the problem.

There are a number of strategies for using data to build a shared understanding of content among your faculty members. One common strategy, as noted above, is for teachers to take, or at least examine, the tests their students take. This practice allows teachers to determine whether standardized tests align with the skills they are teaching. Another strategy is for teachers to photocopy student work on an assignment, grade it individually, and then compare how they evaluated the work with how their peers evaluate it. In both strategies, data are used as a springboard for focused conversations about academic content that the faculty believes is important for students to know and understand.

Conversations like these may lead to questions about the breadth or depth of the curriculum. When looking at disappointing test results, we've heard overwhelmed teachers say, "But that's not in the curriculum!" or "I taught it—they just didn't learn it!" or "There isn't time to teach that." This is a good opportunity to investigate how content areas are addressed in the curriculum based on a question or concern that arises from the data. A group of fourth-grade teachers investigating students' poor performance in reading non-fiction mapped their curriculum projects across the school year and realized that the vast majority of their reading and writing assignments were about fiction. Students had little opportunity to read nonfiction, which teachers agreed was a problem not only because it was on the state test, but also because students needed to be able to read nonfiction well to access information and be independent learners.

Careful investigations of student work usually lead to discussions about work quality. If teachers on your team don't agree on what a high or low level of student performance looks like, it will be hard for your team to identify a meaningful learner-centered problem to address throughout your improvement effort. Investigations into the data may result in different conclusions from different teachers. A common way to address this is to use a rubric—a delineation of the skills and knowledge students need to produce high-quality work. Developing and using rubrics ensures that data analysis is based on a common set of criteria. Rubrics help teachers identify discrete areas of student strengths and weaknesses, which can help point the way to understanding a meaningful problem that can be addressed through action planning. As will be explained in chapter 7, rubrics are also a helpful tool in measuring student progress.

DEVELOPING COMMON LANGUAGE

At the Franklin High School math department meeting, department chair Mallory Golden said, "We keep coming back to complex math questions as posing challenges for kids. We've definitely started to identify the learner-centered problem as one of solving 'multistep math problems,' but I'm not sure I know what we mean by that."

"I think of 'multistep problems' as problems where students need to do more than one mathematical step to answer the question," answered Eddie.

"Oh, I was thinking of it as problems in which students need to use more than one piece of information to answer the question," said Adelina.

As conversations about student work progress, it's important to develop common language to describe a learner-centered problem worthy of your time and energy. At Franklin, though becoming proficient with multistep questions was both a school and state priority, teachers held very different definitions of what constituted a multistep question. When teachers don't take the time to pinpoint exactly what they mean when discussing their learner-centered problem, their findings and consequent actions will be inconsistent at best, and potentially inaccurate.

Important differences in how teachers think about student learning often remain hidden when discussions remain at an abstract level. Teachers may identify "number sense" as a student weakness in math, but do all teachers mean the same thing when they use that phrase? Teachers leave a meeting with the decision that struggling students need more "scaffolding," but do they share an understanding of why students are struggling? If teachers each have a different understanding of the problem, it is more likely that their responses will be inconsistent because, in fact, they are addressing different problems! In order to get to the heart of a problem and systematically improve instruction, it's important to make sure teachers clearly understand one another, as well as the nature of the topic they're exploring.

Groups of teachers develop a common language around teaching and learning in different ways. In some schools, teachers use a common rubric to assess student essays to determine whether they share a common definition of "voice" in narrative writing. In other schools, teachers categorize test questions into conceptual areas and compare their categories. At Clark, teachers noted that students were weakest in the area of "interpretation" on the state test, but didn't know exactly what that meant. The data manager pulled sample "interpretation" questions off the state department of education website. Teachers answered the questions and then discussed the skills needed to answer the questions correctly. In each of these examples, the exchange among teachers is based on work or test items that are in front of them. With this common reference point, the substance of discussions becomes fine-grained, leaves less room for misunderstandings, and offers more opportunities for colleagues to build on one another's insights.

IDENTIFYING THE LEARNER-CENTERED PROBLEM

When teachers are thoughtfully examining data, there are always more questions to ask and more leads to follow. Deeper knowledge about the nature of the problem and how to solve it are the building blocks of your school's theory of how to improve learning and teaching. Much like a research project, in which having a good question can be the driving force behind a strong research process, identifying a meaningful problem to work on can be the driving force behind a strong instructional improvement process.

Data analysis supports a culture of improvement by building the habit of inquiry in which you constantly ask questions and find answers not in your preconceived judgments of children, but in observable data. Therefore, it is critical to invest the time and effort needed to identify a meaningful problem that becomes the focus of the improvement process. On the other hand, waiting too long to act runs the risk of "analysis paralysis." Thus, it is important to realize that you can always conduct additional analyses and examine other types of data.

How do you know when you are ready to identify a learner-centered problem that will drive the improvement process? We've found the following questions to be useful guides:

* Do you have more than a superficial understanding of the reasons behind students' areas of low performance?

* Is there logic—based on the data you have examined—in how and why you've arrived at the specific problem identified?

* Is your understanding of the problem supported by multiple sources of data?

* Did you learn anything new in examining the data?

* Do you all define the problem in the same way?

* Is the problem specifically focused on knowledge and skills you want students to have?

* If you solve this problem, will it help you meet your larger goals for students?

When you can answer "yes" to these questions, you are ready to move to the next step in the improvement process.

5

EXAMINING INSTRUCTION

Elizabeth A. City, Melissa Kagle, and Mark B. Teoh

FRANKLIN MATH DEPARTMENT HEAD MALLORY GOLDEN BEGAN the meeting by acknowledging the department's work: "Well, we've made a lot of progress so far. We've decided that the learning problem is that students are not able to solve multistep problems very well. Now, our next step is to understand why they're having so much trouble with multistep problems."

"Are we really going to talk about this for another meeting?" interrupted Eddie. "All we do is talk. Students are going to fail the state test again while we sit around and talk."

"I hear you," replied Mallory. "But my question is, what's happening—or not happening—in our teaching that's leading our students to struggle with multistep problems?"

"Look, it's not as if we haven't taught multistep problems," responded Eddie. "They're in every book I've used, not to mention on the state test. It would help if kids would do their homework and come prepared to class, but I don't see that happening anytime soon, so I'll give them more multistep problems to work on in class."

Educators are constantly solving problems. These problems range from simple—a student doesn't have a pencil—to complex—a student doesn't understand an assignment or two students aren't getting along. To manage the steady stream of problems, we tend to leap to solutions. However, many of the problems we face are too complicated for us to solve quickly on our own.

The learning problem you have articulated by this step of the improvement cycle is a complicated problem—if it were an easy one, you would have solved it by now. In order to solve the learning problem, you need to understand both the learning and teaching dimensions of the problem. While many factors outside of the school influence childrens' learning, they are outside the reach of most teachers. What we educators do have under our control in schools is teaching. Teaching, therefore, will be the focus of the solutions in the action plan. Before deciding on a plan of action, you must understand what you're doing now, and do so in a way that enables teachers to take responsibility for solving the problem, rather than feeling that it's not their problem or that they can't do anything about it anyway, or that they're being blamed for it.

We have found that reframing the learning problem as a "problem of practice" is critical before proceeding to the action plan.[1] The problem of practice is an expression of the student learning problem and the teaching related to that problem, and is an integration of analysis of both assessment and instructional data. The problem of practice should:

* Include learning and teaching
* Be specific and fine-grained
* Be a problem within the school's control
* Be a problem that, if solved, will mean progress toward some larger goal

Not only does identifying the problem of practice lay important groundwork for future action, it also saves time. While we have seen schools spend as little as four hours or as much as four months examining instruction at this stage of the improvement process, any such investment of time will likely keep you from spending months or years on something that's not going to work because it's not addressing the actual problem of practice.

There are four main tasks to help you investigate instruction and articulate a problem of practice:

1. Link learning and teaching: With this particular learning problem, how does instruction impact what students learn?

2. Develop the skill of examining practice: How do we look at instructional data?

3. Develop a shared understanding of effective practice: What does effective instruction for our learning problem look like and what makes it effective?

4. Analyze current practice: What is actually happening in the classroom in terms of the learning problem, and how does it relate to our understanding of effective practice?

Because learning and teaching are so intertwined, as a school you may already have partially completed one or more of these tasks in your inquiry into the learning problem. While schools that are new to the improvement process may find it easiest to proceed through the steps in sequence, many schools find that examining instruction involves a more simultaneous application of the steps. More important than the order in which the steps are completed is the necessity that they all be addressed.

LINK LEARNING AND TEACHING

Mallory continued the math department meeting by asking teachers to use their experience in the classroom to brainstorm why Franklin students were struggling with multistep problems. Teachers wrote their responses on sticky notes:

Students don't come to high school adequately prepared for complex problems.

Students aren't able to think abstractly.

Students give up when the problem is hard.

The vocabulary on the state math tests is unfamiliar to students.

Students have a math phobia—they think they can't do math.

Students aren't familiar with the format of the state test.

Students have a lot of social and emotional issues.

Students are working after school, and they don't do their homework.

The first step in articulating a problem of practice is to establish a link between learning and teaching. This may sound surprising, since we presumably wouldn't be teachers if we didn't think our efforts mattered for learning. However, in the context of high-stakes testing and the day-to-day pressures of school, it can be easy to forget that teaching matters for learning. If teachers don't fundamentally believe that their teaching can make a difference for student learning, then it's going to be difficult to convince them to change their teaching.

Linking learning and teaching is also about helping teachers take responsibility for student learning. "Responsibility" doesn't mean "it's my fault"—it means "I can and will do something about the student learning problem." Poor test results and external pressures can lead educators to try to shift responsibility to others through finger-pointing and blame. For school-based educators, however, the primary focus has to be on what we have control over—what happens at school. This is not an easy task. Despite their hard work, teachers don't often see great improvements on state tests, and they don't think it's possible to work any harder. They see lots of big issues that affect student learning that they can't readily fix, like poverty, previous learning experiences, and parental education. The school leader must keep the conversation focused on what teachers can do in the classroom.

What we can do is teach well. To improve the quality of teaching in a school, leaders must push the conversation about the learning problem past the level of what students are and aren't doing to look at what teachers are and aren't doing. Additionally, school leaders have to help teachers link learning and teaching in a way that doesn't make them defensive but does get them thinking about their own practice. When planning opportunities for teachers to link learning and teaching, consider these points:

* How will you move the conversation from "students" (or "parents" or "community," etc.) to "teachers"?
* How will you frame the work as an opportunity to improve instruction, rather than as a failure (proactive vs. reactive)?
* How will you help teachers have a questioning rather than a defensive stance?
* How will you surface and get people to acknowledge the fundamental assumption that teaching matters for learning?

Many school leaders we have worked with use structured protocols to address these questions and make the conversation both safer and closer to instruction for teachers. At Franklin, Mallory used the Affinity Protocol [see Selected Protocols at the end of the book] to have teachers brainstorm hypotheses about the student learning problem. After

Mallory saw that most of the sticky notes started with "Students," she encouraged teachers to consider other reasons students might be struggling with multistep problems, and to try starting some ideas with "I" or "Teachers." Teachers' responses included:

There's too much math to teach in a year—no time to spend on long problems.	Parents don't know the math, so they can't help their kids.	Teachers spend most of their time on applying formulas, not on complex problems.	I put multistep problems at the end of assignments, and they are often skipped.
I don't really teach strategies for doing multistep problems.	Teachers spend too much time lecturing at students and doing all the work.	Students don't practice on their own enough.	The math book doesn't have enough multistep problems to practice, and I don't have time to find more.

Although many of their sticky notes still didn't focus specifically on teachers, when they organized all of their notes into categories, they labeled the categories "Curriculum," "Instruction," and "Motivation/Expectations," and added a "Parking Lot" category for things over which they had no control. The process of working through the protocol helped teachers decide that ideas like "Students aren't able to think abstractly" should be in the category of "Instruction," even though they hadn't thought of it that way originally. The categories, which focus on what teachers are doing rather than students, reflected the faculty's evolving understanding of their role in students' learning. We have seen many schools use the Affinity Protocol with great success because it's anonymous (thus letting participants write down things they might not say out loud), it levels the speaking field (thus addressing the potential for one person to dominate or for everyone to wait to see what the principal says), and it's fun (people appreciate the hands-on experience of using sticky notes and moving them around, rather than sitting and talking).

Exhibit 5.1

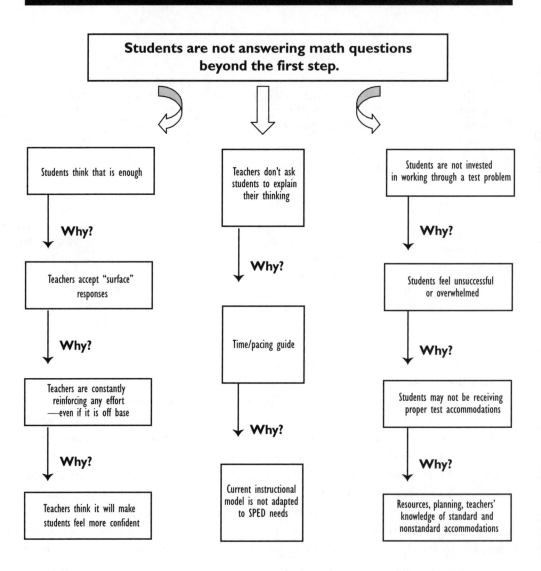

WHY-WHY-WHY SPECIAL EDUCATION SUBGROUP—MATHEMATICS

Students are not answering math questions beyond the first step.

Students think that is enough

Why?

Teachers accept "surface" responses

Why?

Teachers are constantly reinforcing any effort —even if it is off base

Why?

Teachers think it will make students feel more confident

Teachers don't ask students to explain their thinking

Why?

Time/pacing guide

Why?

Current instructional model is not adapted to SPED needs

Students are not invested in working through a test problem

Why?

Students feel unsuccessful or overwhelmed

Why?

Students may not be receiving proper test accommodations

Why?

Resources, planning, teachers' knowledge of standard and nonstandard accommodations

Other schools use a process of asking "why?" repeatedly to peel away the layers of the learning problem. They start with their student learning problem and then ask why they have that problem. For each answer they come up with, they ask why again, and repeat that process several times. One middle school's "why-why-why" diagram about their special education students who were not answering math questions beyond the first step is displayed in Exhibit 5.1.[2]

The initial step of linking learning and teaching need not take a long time—most schools we know devote one meeting to it. However, it lays the groundwork for closer examination of practice by focusing attention squarely on the instructional core,[3] which is defined as the interaction between teachers, students, and content. The data used in the protocols above are teachers' own experiences, including their assumptions and beliefs. This is a good place to start because this type of data is easily accessible and influences how teachers approach the problem of practice. To truly understand the problem of practice, however, you will have to get closer to teachers' actual practice.

DEVELOP THE SKILL OF EXAMINING PRACTICE

At Clark, teachers had spent the previous few weeks doing peer observations, with each teacher visiting one colleague. In grade-level team meetings, teachers shared what they had seen.

"I really enjoyed visiting Anita's classroom. I saw students who were really engaged," began Kristina, a third-grade teacher.

"That was true in Jae's classroom, too," said Vivian, a fourth-grade teacher. "Students were well-behaved, they worked well in groups, and they looked like they were really on task."

"Good," replied Sandy. "Engagement is important. The next question is, what evidence did you see that students were engaged, and what task were students engaged in?"

Examining practice is a complex undertaking. Examiners need to be able to recognize, understand, and describe what they're seeing. This is not as easy as it sounds. Most teachers have not had much experience with examining teaching, which means they have neither the skills to describe teaching in a fine-grained, evidence-based way, nor the collegial culture in which examining practice feels supportive rather than threatening. If you plunge right into examining instruction without developing skills for doing so, you will find the conversation is awash in compliments and generalities like "students are engaged" and "the lesson was well-planned." One principal we know calls this "happy talk"—our tendency as educators to be overly nice to colleagues, especially when we're just beginning to examine practice. Although it is often helpful to point out what is working well, that level of generality and abstraction does little to help us understand how our teaching links to the learning in the classroom. Developing skills for examining practice is not something you need to spend a long time doing. Spending even one meeting developing these skills will help faculty move beyond happy talk to precise discussions of teaching when carefully examining the instruction in your school.

Similar to examining student work, a careful examination of teacher work relies on the following qualities:

* Evidence
* Precise, shared vocabulary
* Collaborative conversation with explicit norms

The first and most critical component of examining instruction is evidence—in other words, data about teaching. There are many possibilities for instructional data, ranging from artifacts, such as assignments or assessments, to observations, such as classroom visits or video tapes, to self-reports, such as surveys or interviews of teachers.

Developing the discipline of noting and talking about evidence takes practice. One principal we know calls it "learning to see." She shows her teachers videos of teaching (not of teachers within her building) and asks them to note what they see. She models using language like "I noticed that . . ." "I saw that . . ." "I heard that . . ." with examples of what she saw and heard. With her persistent reminders to cite evidence rather than rushing to judgments, teachers quickly develop the habit of doing so, and then use this skill to examine their own practice when they observe each other teach.

The second component of examining practice is precise, shared vocabulary. It is important that teachers be able to specify what they see in language that is understandable to others. This habit can be developed through experience with responding to observations. For example, a teacher who has not had much practice analyzing instruction might observe a teacher introducing a new math concept and respond with the comment, "I noticed that students seem confused." "Confused," like "engaged," could mean many things to different teachers. In contrast, a more precise observation might be, "I noticed that several students didn't start the assignment immediately. One student was looking at other students. Two students were talking to each other while looking at the assignment, and four students raised their hands after the teacher gave directions for the assignment."

The third component of examining instruction is collaborative conversation with explicit norms. It is more powerful to observe and analyze practice collaboratively because each person brings their own set of beliefs and assumptions to the observation. Hearing others' responses to the same lesson helps challenge individual assumptions, helps us notice different things and see the same things in a new way, and leads to a better understanding of the practice observed.

In order to make the conversation both more productive and safer, groups who are examining practice together should articulate and write down their norms. As discussed in chapter 1, "norms" are ground rules for discussion. Groups should consider whether there are any norms they need in order to be willing to discuss their own teaching. An important norm is that of confidentiality, that what is discussed about an observation will not be shared outside the group doing the analysis. Also, as mentioned above, it is important that observations be backed up by evidence. If this is a norm, members of the group can push each other to back up their assertions with evidence from the classroom.

To develop these skills of examining practice, schools we have worked with use strategies such as watching videotape of their own or other teachers. Videotape of teaching from outside the school is an especially useful strategy for schools where observing each other is still too threatening. Observing and discussing the practice of teachers they don't know gives teachers the opportunity to build the skills necessary for safe and insightful conversations about practice. We have also seen schools develop these skills when one brave soul, such as a teacher or instructional coach, volunteers to have other teachers observe his teaching and they then discuss their observations, practicing using evidence, precise vocabulary, and norms. It can be especially compelling when the school leader volunteers to have teachers observe and discuss her teaching, thus opening her own practice to her faculty for examination.

This step of "learning to see" instruction focuses on description rather than evaluation. The distinction is important because our normative judgments tend to cloud our ability to see what's happening—for example, students look "engaged," which we think is "good," but when we look at what they're "engaged" with, we see that they're doing work that's several grade levels below where they should be. There are limits, though, to what describing can do.

DEVELOP A SHARED UNDERSTANDING OF EFFECTIVE PRACTICE

At Clark, a seventh-grade teacher had volunteered to have colleagues observe her teaching the concept of inference. At the next faculty meeting, teachers were discussing what they had seen and were thinking about teaching inference.

"The kids were doing inference through drama," said Vivian. "First, they were taking lines from everyday interactions, like 'I'm fine' or 'Excuse me,' and they were saying the lines in all different ways, and then the rest of the class was guessing—or inferring—what they were actually thinking when they said it. One student said "Excuse me" like she was really embarrassed, and another said it like he was really annoyed. Then they moved on to reading lines from *A Midsummer Night's Dream,* and they worked on saying those lines with meaning that was appropriate, based on the text."

"It was great, but I hope there are other ways to teach inferring—I'm just not the drama type and I can't see using Shakespeare with third graders," Kristina said. "Do we have any other ideas about teaching inference?"

A critical step in articulating a problem of practice is to develop a shared understanding of instruction that will effectively address the learning problem your school has identified. We need a vision for what this effective teaching looks like so we can assess whether what we're doing now fits or doesn't fit that vision. The problem of practice is in the gap between current practice and effective practice for addressing the learning problem. If an understanding of effective practice for addressing the learning problem already existed among your faculty, you probably wouldn't have the learning problem, as teachers would know how to successfully teach inferring or solving multistep problems, or whatever your learning problem is. Thus, building teacher knowledge is important in articulating the problem of practice. The faculty will continue to develop and refine their understanding of effective practice as they develop the action plan, implement the action plan, and assess progress, but it's important to lay the groundwork at this stage. Without a vision of what's possible, we limit our expectations and goals for addressing the learning problem, as well as our ability to examine our own practice with an informed eye.

DRAWING ON INTERNAL RESOURCES

In developing a shared understanding of effective practice, the essential question is, Based on student and teacher data, what does instruction that addresses the learning problem look like? To answer this question, schools can look internally at instruction in their own buildings and look externally to other practitioners and to research. Looking internally has advantages: it honors the work of teachers in the building, which can build a sense of confidence and competence, and the practice is very specific to the context of the school, thus requiring less translation or adaptation than an external practice might. Looking internally also has potential disadvantages: the scope of ideas may be narrow because we may not have all the best answers; singling out particular teachers as examples of "effective practice" may promote a sense of competition or comparison among teachers; and our assumptions about what's possible may be limited. A school that chooses to use examples of effective practice from inside the school can mitigate these pitfalls in several ways. First, introduce a wider range of practices by bringing in outside resources, such as journal articles that address the learning problem. Second, involve the whole staff in identifying effective practice to cut down on feelings of competition. And third, facilitate conversations carefully to get teachers thinking more widely about practice.

When looking internally to develop ideas of effective practice, the key is to ground the discussion in evidence. We know many schools where teachers share instructional strategies, which are called best practices. This is an important way to develop craft knowledge, but is often disconnected from data and from the learning problem. Some schools we work with address this by inviting teachers to share practices related to the learning problem and to support the belief that they are "best" practices with evidence of student learning. In these schools, teachers use the following protocol: "This is a 'best practice' because when I did this, the learning looked like this." They then present their instructional strategy and evidence from student work. Connecting best practices to data serves multiple purposes: it increases the likelihood that the practice is effective rather than simply congenial; it reinforces the discipline of grounding all conversations about teaching and learning in evidence rather than generalities or assumptions; it's more persuasive—teachers are more likely to try something for which there's evidence that it works; and it reinforces the link between learning and teaching.

DRAWING ON EXTERNAL RESOURCES

At Franklin, Sasha, the math coach, showed the math department videos of algebra lessons from Japan, Germany, and the United States from the TIMSS (Trends in International Math and Science Study).

"Well, sure, it would be great if our lessons looked like the Japanese one, but our classrooms are really different," Eddie said. "First of all, we're dealing with a much more diverse population than those Japanese teachers are. Second of all, I've tried that approach of putting a problem on the board and having kids work on it, and it just doesn't work. Some of them don't even start it, and just talk to their neighbors. Others start it, and then stop as soon as they're stuck. If I'm not helping them through each step of the problem, they just give up."

"What do you see in these videos that relates to the article that I gave you about differences in teaching practice across countries at different performance levels on international math tests?" asked Sasha.

"The article said that countries in the middle of the pack, like the U.S. and Germany, tend to spend lots of class time on reviewing homework and applying formulas. We definitely saw that in the video," said Mallory.

"The article also said that the countries that score higher, like Japan, have students develop some understanding of the theory behind an operation, rather than just applying an algorithm. And there was the piece in the article about breadth vs. depth—U.S. textbooks are much fatter than Japanese and Korean textbooks and cover a lot more concepts. We saw some of both of those things. In the U.S. classroom, students were doing many problems that drew on a number of different math concepts, whereas in the Japanese classroom, students did two problems in the class period, both on the same math concepts."

"Okay," said Eddie. "Like I said, I'd love to teach just like those Japanese teachers. But how do you think it would work in our situation?"

In schools, internal resources often are not adequate for developing a shared understanding of effective practice related to the student learning problem. This is when school leaders should use external resources to seed the conversation about effective practice and build teachers' knowledge. You can go to the source, by visiting another school or attending a professional conference, or you can bring it in, by learning from consultants or reviewing research. Looking externally brings its own advantages and disadvantages. Among the advantages are bringing in a range of ideas and expertise that is beyond that of your staff, and making it easier to have an "objective" conversation. Many school leaders we know bring in articles and videos to start conversations with their faculty, which helps teachers get perspective on their own practice and talk about "effective practice." External resources also can challenge assumptions about what's possible by showing evidence of other practitioners succeeding where we have not; provide access to ideas that have potentially been tested more systematically or for a longer period of time (e.g., research); and help triangulate teachers' hunches and experiences of good practice with external ideas.

Drawing on external resources also brings potential disadvantages. For some teachers, external resources challenge their professionalism and suggest that they're not good teachers or don't know what good teaching is. There is also the "But they're different! That wouldn't work here!" problem, as math teacher Eddie exemplified at Franklin. In this view, educators assume that whatever success the external resource had won't hold when applied to their own unique setting. With external resources, it's not always clear which elements are essential and which can be adapted (or how) to your context.

Adopting an inquiry stance in which any resource—internal or external—is questioned and investigated addresses these disadvantages. Inquiry is essential in developing a shared understanding of effective practice because you want everyone to understand not only what effective practice for the learning problem looks like but why it is effective. In the Clark example about using Shakespeare to teach inferring, teachers need to move beyond simply deciding that drama is a good tool for teaching inferring to inquire why drama seems to be effective. Is it because students have the opportunity to use nontext clues like body language and intonation to interpret text? Or is it because the Shakespearean text is so difficult that students have to figure out ways to make sense of the text? Or is it because of the kinds of questions the teacher asked? Similarly, in the Franklin example, is the Japanese math teacher's practice effective because he is helping students understand theory instead of applying an algorithm, because he allows students to solve the problem in different ways, or because, as the research suggests, he is going into more depth and covering less content? As teachers ask and answer these questions, they'll form a vision of effective practice that they can adapt to fit their own setting, but one that is consistent with key elements that make practice effective. This depth of understanding will support both their examination of practice and their implementation of it later on in the improvement process.

Some schools form inquiry groups in which teachers frame a question about teaching to their learning problem and then investigate resources to help them answer the question. At Clark, teachers inquired about "Think Alouds,"[4] the process of teachers making their own thinking explicit for students as they modeled a strategy or skill, like inferring. In one high school, teachers wanted to know how to help their students who were several years below grade level in reading catch up to grade-level reading. They particularly wanted strategies that were both effective and age-appropriate for their students, and no one on the faculty knew what to do. The teachers formed an inquiry group in which they found, read, and discussed several articles and books on the subject. After a lengthy discussion, they generated a list of effective practices for helping students significantly behind in reading.

It often helps to draw on both internal and external resources. Some people are more persuaded by research, others by a colleague's success, while some people have to see the effectiveness of a practice to both believe and understand it. Very often, we need a combination of research, practices, and experience to develop our understanding of effective practice. At one elementary school, the faculty thought that differentiated instruction might be a good strategy for meeting needs of various learners, but didn't know what it would look like. They read articles, watched videos, listened to their special education teachers describe their practice, and discussed all of the ideas to develop a common understanding of differentiated instruction as it applied in their particular context.

ANALYZE CURRENT PRACTICE

At Franklin, the math teachers had decided to focus their next faculty meeting on exploring three questions formed by both their brainstorm about why students were struggling with multistep problems and their investigation into effective practice: 1) Are we teaching a consistent strategy for solving multistep problems? 2) Do we give students sufficient practice with multistep problems? 3) How do we support students in believing that they can do well with complex problems? Now they had to decide how they were going to answer those questions.

Sasha, the math coach, suggested that they observe each other teaching to get a sense of what was being done in different classrooms.

Eddie disagreed. "I'm not giving up my planning period to observe people teaching. I need my planning time."

Mallory countered, "Well, Roger might be able to get subs to cover so we can see each other."

"I don't want to miss teaching a class so that I can go observe other people, either. I'm behind where I need to be with the kids as it is. Besides, do we really need to see each other teach to answer these questions? I think it's safe to say we're not teaching a consistent strategy for solving multistep problems—I have no idea how anyone else teaches them. Do we give students sufficient practice? Well, I don't know what 'sufficient' is, but apparently it's not enough or they'd be doing better. And we tell students they can do the problems if they'll try."

In order to articulate a problem of practice, faculty must be able to describe what is going on currently in the school, with a shared understanding of effective practice as the referent point. Gathering data about teaching to examine what's happening in classrooms helps move the conversation away from an emotional blame game and toward identifying the teaching dimensions of a problem of practice. Just as we can think students have learned something until we look at their work and see otherwise, as teachers, so can we think we've taught something until we look at our work and see otherwise.

As with any effort to use data wisely, when examining instruction, school leaders face many decisions about what data to look at and how to look at it. These decisions come with trade-offs and depend heavily on the context of particular schools. The data that may help one school understand their teaching practice as it relates to their learning problem may not help another school at all, or may take so long to collect and analyze that the energy for improvement dwindles and no action is ever taken. Three questions to consider when making decisions about how to examine instruction are:

* What data will answer your questions about teaching practice in your school?
* What are teachers ready for and willing to do?
* What are your resources, including time?

WHAT DATA WILL ANSWER YOUR QUESTIONS ABOUT TEACHING PRACTICE IN YOUR SCHOOL?

As discussed in chapter 3, decisions about what data to look at should start with questions. In the case of teaching practice, it's critical to frame what questions you have about what's happening in classrooms related to the student learning problem. If you don't, you're likely to collect lots of data that don't help you. This can waste precious time, as well as good will about engaging in the process of using data, particularly around something as sensitive as teaching practice. The questions should draw on your inquiry up to this point, including your understanding of effective practice. We know one school that approaches describing current practice as an instructional audit. The faculty develops a list of questions related to things they would expect to see in classrooms effectively teaching to the learning problem, and then observe each other teaching, taking notes on the answers to those questions. We have also seen schools use the Question Formulation Technique mentioned in chapter 3 to formulate questions, and we have seen schools fill out a simple grid:

Exhibit 5.2

EXPLORING THE STUDENT LEARNING PROBLEM		
Statement of Student Learning Problem:_____		
Why are students having the learning problem?	What questions do we have?	What data will help us answer our questions?

The questions will determine what the relevant data are. For example, if the prevailing chorus from teachers is, "I'm teaching it—they're just not learning it," a question might be whether teachers are actually teaching whatever "it" is. The data needed to answer this question will most likely involve seeing teachers actually teach. If the question is what kinds of tasks we ask students to do related to the learning problem, the data involved might be homework and classwork assignments, tests, and other assessments. If the question is about what teachers think they're doing, helpful data would come from asking teachers to describe their practice through surveys, focus groups, or interviews.

One elementary school investigating problem-solving in math met in cross-grade groups to try to understand their lowest-performing students' experience of a constructivist math curriculum. Teachers wondered if more structure was needed in the lessons for the most struggling students. If so, what was the best method, what would it look like, and when should they introduce it? After sharing lesson plans and student work, teachers decided to observe in each others' classrooms to get more data on the classroom performance of this neediest group of students and the instruction in the classrooms. Each teacher arranged to observe a peer before the next meeting. They then shared their observations to determine patterns of response and brainstorm the kinds of support they felt their students needed, based on the observation data they'd collected from their own and their peers' students.

Another school devoted several staff meetings to something called triads. The principal divided the staff into groups of three, mixing up specialists and teachers of different grade levels. Each triad came up with a focused question they wanted to investigate, such as a question about teaching inference in reading. Teachers were then released from team meetings in order to observe their colleagues and collect data in response to the question posed by their colleagues. At the next meeting, faculty met in their triads to share observation data and reflect on what they'd learned.

WHAT ARE TEACHERS READY FOR AND WILLING TO DO?

The next step is to figure out what sorts of data teachers are ready and willing to examine about their own practice. Two helpful questions to consider: Are teachers accustomed to being in each other's classrooms, having people watch them teach, and discussing their practice? Is there a culture of learning where talking about teaching practice is seen as an opportunity to improve rather than an evaluation? If the answer to these questions is "yes," then all data about teaching practice is a possibility, including data that come from directly observing teaching, like videotape and class visits. If the answer is "no," then direct observation data may be too threatening to teachers and they may refuse to do it, or be so general in their observations that the data aren't helpful. In this case, data that rely on self-reports from teachers, such as surveys, focus groups, or interviews, can be less threatening, provide information, and begin to get teachers accustomed to the idea of examining their practice. If the answer is somewhere in between, then examining artifacts of teaching such as student or teacher work may be appropriate.

At an elementary school where math scores on the state test were low and teachers weren't comfortable having someone watch them teach, the instructional leadership team designed a survey based on their questions about what was happening with math. The teachers on the team made a special point of distributing and collecting the survey themselves without involvement from the principal, because they hoped teachers would answer more honestly if the questions came from other teachers. The team learned several important things when they analyzed the results from the survey: Teachers weren't spending the 60 minutes per day they were supposed to on math, teachers generally didn't use the manipulatives that were part of the curriculum, and teachers wanted more support in how to teach math well.

In many schools, custom or contract will dictate the extent of and the guidelines for observing teachers in classrooms. We have found that schools that use questions and data to establish a culture of inquiry in which teachers are participants rather than targets find ways to examine practice. Teachers want to know the answers to the questions they have generated, and thus are more likely to participate in collecting the data and examining their own practice.

WHAT ARE YOUR RESOURCES, INCLUDING TIME?

Finally, resources—especially time—play a role in determining what data you decide to examine. Again, two questions: How much time do you have to collect and analyze the data about instruction? What other resources do you have available to you? The answers to these questions influence how many data sources you can examine and which ones you choose. If, like Franklin, you are under intense pressure to take action and you only have a couple of meetings available in which to examine instruction, you might choose to look at artifacts of teaching and hear self-reports through a focus group. If, like Clark, you have less urgency and more regular meetings available, you might choose a more lengthy process, such as teacher and administrator observations in classrooms. Other resources will influence your choices as well. Do you have someone who can collect and do initial analysis of the data? If not, you may not want to do a survey, which is quick for teachers to complete but takes time to compile and analyze. Do you have a way to free teachers to visit each others' classrooms? Some schools use combinations of substitute teachers, administrators, and teachers who have a planning period to cover for other teachers who are visiting my colleagues' classrooms. Other schools have limited resources in terms of time and people, but use technology to support their data efforts. We've seen schools use electronic polling tools like www.surveymonkey.com to do a survey of their teachers (and their students, too).

A primary resource in examining instruction is you, the school leader. While you want teachers involved in examining practice at some level, teachers very often will not be able to examine practice across the whole school. You have the distinct advantage of flexibility and time. Though it may not seem that you can get into classrooms as much as you would like, you do not have the responsibility of being in a single classroom in fixed periods for most of the day. Thus, you have the opportunity to visit multiple classrooms, attend different grade-level and content-area meetings, and get a sense of the bigger picture of what's happening across classrooms.

TRADE-OFFS

With all of these decisions there are trade-offs. If you examine instruction more quickly with limited data sources, you will get to designing and implementing solutions faster, but you may sacrifice some accuracy in understanding the teaching dimensions of the problem of practice. If you take your time and examine several data sources, you may be more accurate, but you may lose a sense of urgency and momentum for improvement. If you tread carefully and don't push too hard on teachers' comfort level about examining practice, you may get willing participants, but you may not get the level of precision and depth you want in the problem of practice. Push too hard, and you may get resistance when you go to implement solutions. If you have a few people do most of the examining instruction work, you may get it done more quickly and at greater depth, but you may not get the level of understanding and buy-in you'll want from the rest of the teachers whose practice you ultimately want to improve. As a leader, you have to balance your questions, your teachers' skills and readiness, and your resources with the goal of answering your questions as thoroughly as possible in the time frame you have.

ARTICULATING THE PROBLEM OF PRACTICE

Once you have linked learning and teaching, developed the skill of examining practice, developed a shared understanding of effective practice, and analyzed current practice in your school, you can articulate the problem of practice that will be the focus of your improvement efforts. At Clark, the problem of practice is: "Students have trouble drawing text-based inference when reading. Teachers do not teach inference explicitly, and do not help students make connections between the inferences they make in their lives and the inferences they need to make from text." At Franklin, the problem of practice is: "Students do not solve multistep math problems well and do not work independently on math problems well. Teachers do not consistently teach a process for solving multistep problems, and they don't give students enough opportunities to work with multistep problems." After articulating a problem of practice, you are ready to design an action plan to solve the problem.

SECTION **III** **ACT**

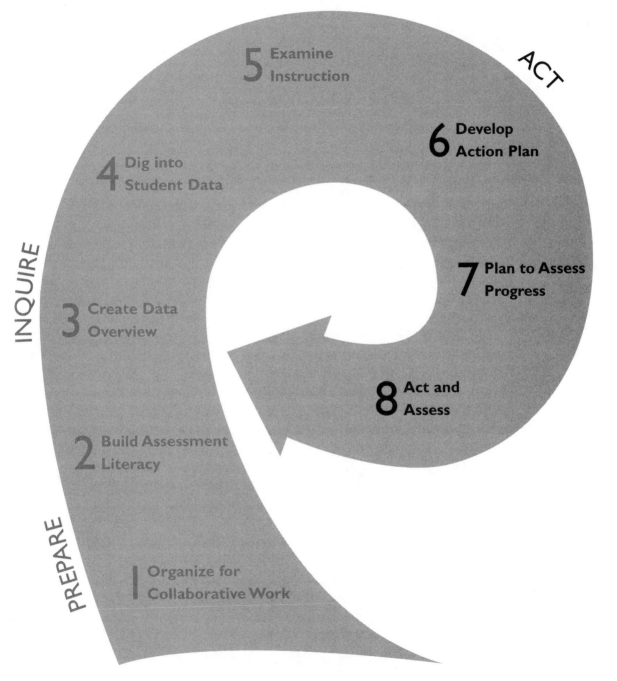

ACT

5 Examine Instruction

6 Develop Action Plan

4 Dig into Student Data

INQUIRE

7 Plan to Assess Progress

3 Create Data Overview

8 Act and Assess

2 Build Assessment Literacy

PREPARE

1 Organize for Collaborative Work

6

DEVELOPING AN ACTION PLAN

Tom Buffett, Mark B. Teoh, and Gerardo Martinez

CLARK'S THIRD- AND FOURTH-GRADE TEAM LEADER, ANITA Suarez, found it hard to interrupt her colleagues' animated conversation. "I used that current-events activity that we read about last week," Vivian was saying. "The kids loved it. I often have a hard time getting them interested in a nonfiction reading exercise, but this time they were really into it."

"Well, I tried that 'Think Aloud' thing we saw you do in your classroom," Jae told Vivian. "You know, when you put that poem on the overhead projector and then you walked the kids through what was going on in your head as you read? Well, I don't know how you made it look so easy . . . I could only keep it going for a few minutes before it kind of started feeling like a monologue."

It was encouraging to see the teachers trying out some of the new ideas that had come out of their work together. But so far, the efforts were individualized and uncoordinated. As leader of her team, Anita knew that she would be responsible for helping them come up with a coherent plan for making instructional changes together. But she hadn't led this kind of work before, and she wondered how she could channel her team's energy into getting a formal plan down on paper.

The third- and fourth-grade team at the Clark K-8 School has deepened its knowledge about effective reading instruction by observing team members teach, discussing professional literature on this subject, and watching and debriefing a video related to literacy instruction. In the process, the team has identified some promising strategies for helping students learn how to make text-based inferences. Like Anita at the Clark School, you may find that teachers at your school begin to improve their instruction as a result of participating in these kinds of activities.

Nevertheless, explicitly committing to a particular strategy or set of strategies for instructional improvement and writing up a formal action plan is important. Creating an action plan will increase the clarity and transparency of your work. You can use the document for communication within your school, and between your school and key external constituents such as families, the district office, and foundations. By committing your team's thinking to paper, you create a process through which team members can raise and address the different understandings that naturally develop when discussing practice. And perhaps most importantly, action planning is a way to translate what you learn through analyzing a broad swath of data—from state test scores to current instructional practices—into concrete strategies for improving what is happening in classrooms.

Successful action planning typically includes the following four tasks:

1. *Decide on an instructional strategy* or strategies that will solve the problem of practice you identified through your analysis of student and teacher data. The instructional strategy your team commits to is the heart of the action plan.

2. *Agree on what your plan will look like in classrooms.* Your team can reach a shared understanding of the strategy by carefully describing what team members would expect to see teachers and students doing if the plan were implemented well.

3. *Put the plan down on paper.* By documenting team members' roles and responsibilities and specifying the concrete steps that need to occur, you build internal accountability for making the plan work. Identifying the professional development time and instruction your team will need and including it in your action plan lets teachers know they will be supported through the process of instructional improvement.

4. *Plan how you will know if the plan is working.* Before implementing your plan, it is important to determine what type of student outcome data you will need to collect in order to understand whether students are indeed learning more. Because this task represents a substantial undertaking that is often overlooked in schools, we discuss it as the sole topic of chapter 7, "Planning to Assess Progress."

As with all of the steps of the improvement process, working together to create an instructional action plan that you will collaboratively implement can help build a professional community at your school. But it isn't easy. This chapter highlights key aspects of each of the first three action-planning tasks listed above and identifies some of the opportunities and tensions that may arise during this phase of the improvement process.

DECIDE ON AN INSTRUCTIONAL STRATEGY

Solutions at last! If you are new to the improvement process recommended by this book, it may seem as though you have had to work through quite a number of steps before turning to the task of deciding what to do about the student learning difficulties you unearthed in data analysis. Now that you have reached this task, however, it is worth the time to deliberately consider possible solutions by first clarifying the scope of your plan, then brainstorming a list of good ideas, and, finally, deciding which of the ideas makes the most sense to implement.

CLARIFY THE SCOPE OF YOUR PLAN

The scope of the plan your team develops will depend upon the "unit" of improvement the team seeks to address. The term "unit" in this case refers to the group that is the subject of your proposed improvement, whether that is a content area, a grade level, the whole building, or some other grouping at your school. Which unit you choose depends on the scope of the problem of practice. When the data show that the problem of practice is consistent across the school, a schoolwide solution makes sense. On the other hand, when the data indicate that the problem of practice is particular to a content area, grade level, or group of students and teachers, a more directed solution will be appropriate. Note, however, that if the unit of improvement you select is smaller than the whole school, your action plan must fit within the context of a whole-school strategy for improvement. In other words, there should be a connection between the smaller unit's action plan and the school's overall approach to improvement so that any success you achieve in solving the problem of practice in the smaller unit also serves a larger schoolwide goal.[1]

At the Clark School, the principal asked each grade-level team to work together to create their own action plan that would support the schoolwide goal of improving student reading performance. At Franklin High School, the principal asked the entire math department to work together to develop a plan that would be implemented in all math classes across all grade levels. The instructional leadership team at one school we have worked with identified the problem of practice as the fact that teachers weren't adequately supporting students in becoming critical thinkers and independent learners. Rather than choose schoolwide strategies that would apply across all classrooms, the team defined the units of improvement as literacy (which is taught by English language arts, social studies, and science teachers) and math. The team then prepared separate action plans for each unit that were both very specific to those content areas and addressed the schoolwide goal of teaching students to be thinkers and independent learners.

School leaders should also consider other factors, such as the availability of resources and faculty capacity, when determining the appropriate scope for their action plans. Some schools we know choose to designate the whole school as the unit of improvement because they do not have the resources to provide adequate support to multiple units when each unit is pursuing a different plan. Other schools we know conduct a pilot action plan with a single grade-level team or content area to test the plan before investing in bringing it to the whole school. We've also seen school leaders use the pilot strategy when they don't think all of the teachers in the unit are prepared to participate. Teachers may not be ready to carry out an action plan because they are already involved in other improvement work and can't take on anything else. Some teachers need to see the action plan working in their own school with their own students before they'll alter their practice, while others who may be new to the school or teaching need to master a few basics (like classroom management or understanding the curriculum) before they introduce strategies from the action plan into their daily work. Conversely, we've seen school leaders choose the whole school as the unit of improvement precisely because many teachers were reluctant or not quite ready, and the whole-school approach made the selected problem of practice everyone's problem instead of the concern of only the willing.

School leaders must weigh all of these considerations. As you think about the scope of action planning in the context of your school, be aware of the potential tension involved in identifying a strategy that is both broad enough to be relevant to teachers who teach different content or students in different grades, and specific enough to ground instructional conversations and improvement efforts in concrete classroom practices.

BRAINSTORM SOLUTIONS TO THE PROBLEM

Even schools we know that are very skilled at examining data and identifying the problem of practice can get stuck at the point of figuring out how to solve the problem. As one principal said to us, "Now what do I do? We know what the problem is, but if we knew what to do about it, we'd have done it already." Looking for solutions can involve engaging teachers in a conversation about how to address a problem, identifying and making creative use of in-house expertise, and being honest about when it is time to seek guidance from outside sources. It is also an opportunity to give teachers time and space to create something collaboratively that is larger and more powerful than anything they could do individually. Developing a shared understanding of effective practice among your faculty, as described in chapter 5, will help generate ideas about appropriate solutions to your problem of practice.

As with all steps of the improvement process, generating solutions is both an end and a means—it is important to come up with the best possible solutions for your problem, but how you come up with those solutions matters, too. Some schools choose to spend more time than others in developing solutions in order to help faculty "buy in" to those solutions. Such buy-in is necessary because the faculty will be the ones implementing the solutions.

There are a number of approaches that you can use to identify possible solutions. The simplest approach is to assemble a group and ask people to brainstorm ideas, which you can keep track of on poster paper or an overhead projector. You can also use a variation of the Affinity Protocol discussed in the previous chapter, where individuals use Post-it Notes to capture their proposed solutions and then work together to group them into logical categories. One school leader we know used a Café Protocol[2] in which faculty discussed possible solutions in small groups at a number of tables in the library. The protocol called for teachers to switch groups twice, each time bringing the solutions from the previous conversation to their new group. At the end of the protocol, the faculty compiled the list of suggestions their conversations had generated. Although the protocol took a full hour, the conversations went much deeper into discussing possible solutions than a brainstorming session would have and allowed faculty to really talk with each other, a change of pace that many of them appreciated.

A few days after the November math department meeting, department chair Mallory Golden met with Sasha Chang, the district math coach assigned to Franklin High School. "So," Mallory explained, "we talked about designing a formal process for solving problems, and teachers got really excited thinking about how we could ask students in all classes to create posters demonstrating their use of this process in solving complex problems. People seemed pretty enthusiastic about teaching a consistent method across classes, and we are going to talk about it more at our next meeting." Mallory paused for a moment. "Frankly," she continued, "I have to say I'm a bit worried we're going to get bogged down in agreeing on the wording of the method and we'll never quite get to using it with the kids."

Like Mallory, many school leaders find that after taking the first important steps toward defining a solution, their faculty may need some guidance about how to operationalize it.

After hearing Mallory's concern, the math coach shared with her a diagram of a process she adapted from George Polya's book, *How to Solve It* (see Exhibit 6.1).[3] The coach had used this particular approach successfully at other schools. Mallory felt it was just what the team needed to make progress on defining their solution, so she asked Sasha to bring her diagram of the Problem-Solving Approach to the next department meeting and talk about how she had used it with other schools. When Sasha did this, the faculty was quite interested in the approach, and by the end of the meeting had decided to adopt it instead of spending any more time trying to reinvent the proverbial wheel.

It is doubtful that the teachers at Franklin High would have embraced the Problem-Solving Approach if someone from the district's central office had mandated it at the beginning of the school year. But because the teachers learned about the approach after they had identified the problem of practice and began to look for solutions, they received the idea enthusiastically. Many school leaders find that a successful search for solutions involves allowing faculty to offer their own suggestions while at the same time planting good ideas from outside sources.

SELECT A SOLUTION TO IMPLEMENT

> Anita posted the list of teaching strategies the Clark third- and fourth-grade team had brainstormed at their previous meeting and told the team they had to decide what solutions they were going to implement. "It looks like a great list to me," said Jae. "I think we should do all of them!" "I don't know about that," Kristina countered. "That list looks overwhelming to me. Why don't we just do one thing well—maybe something straightforward, like working on vocabulary words related to inferring?"

Successful teams are clear about why they select particular strategies. Two important criteria for selecting strategies are the feasibility of implementing the strategy and its likely impact. The feasibility of a particular approach depends on the availability of resources. Commonly required resources for implementing improvement strategies include professional development materials (such as videotapes relating to specific content areas or instructional techniques), support (including workshops and internal or external people who can teach and provide ongoing guidance about the strategy), and time (which might include common planning time or an early-release schedule). The feasibility of any approach also depends on teachers' existing skills and capacities. One capacity that deserves particular mention is the degree of trust that exists among the faculty members. Simply put, some of the most promising strategies for instructional improvement are feasible only if the faculty members trust each other enough to open their classrooms and learn from one another.

Exhibit 6.1

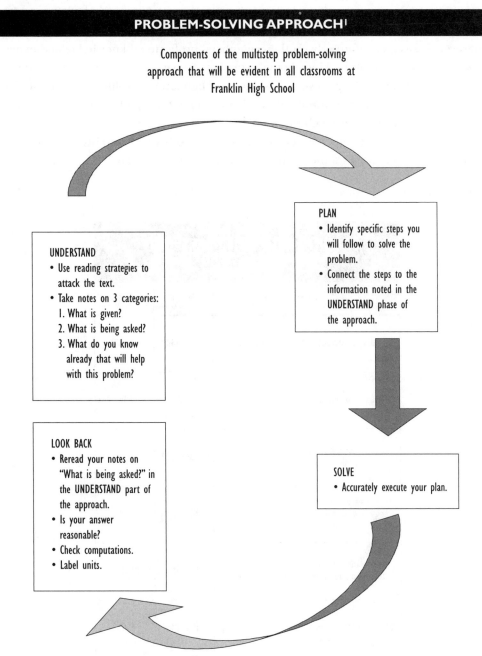

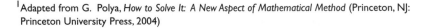

[1] Adapted from G. Polya, *How to Solve It: A New Aspect of Mathematical Method* (Princeton, NJ: Princeton University Press, 2004)

Teams can assess the likely impact of potential strategies in a variety of ways, including reviewing academic research and examining student performance data from other places that are already implementing the strategy in question. As a practical matter, however, teams most often rely on their members' professional knowledge and experience. One useful way of thinking about the impact of a particular strategy is to challenge your faculty to identify "high-leverage" solutions. High-leverage solutions are those that, because of their intensity or the sheer number of students they affect, are likely to make the biggest difference in what children learn.

Clark's third- and fourth-grade team assessed both the feasibility and potential impact of their potential solutions on the chart shown in Exhibit 6.2.

Exhibit 6.2

CLARK K-8 SCHOOL ASSESSMENT OF INFERENCE STRATEGIES

Strategy	Impact	Feasibility
Develop students' inference vocabulary	LOW-MEDIUM	HIGH
Adopt new curriculum that we read about	HIGH	LOW
Think Aloud about inferring (make our thinking explicit)	MEDIUM-HIGH	HIGH
Draw on ways that students already know how to make inferences to teach them what inference is	MEDIUM	HIGH
Use literature that is relevant and meaningful to students to model the inference process	MEDIUM	MEDIUM
Ask open-ended questions that promote inferring	MEDIUM	HIGH

Though teachers agreed that the new curriculum solution might have the greatest potential impact on the chart, the team concluded that this option was not feasible because there were not enough funds in the school's budget. Instead, the Clark School selected from among the strategies that were both feasible and likely to have an impact, and decided to adopt the strategy of using regular Think Alouds as part of their reading instruction.

At schools that have not developed a collaborative orientation toward continuous instructional improvement, teachers will often identify "solutions" that do not involve a change in their instruction. For example, it is common for teachers at schools that lack such a professional community to propose an afterschool program as the key strategy for addressing student weaknesses. While we have seen schools use afterschool programs very effectively as part of their improvement strategy, such programs are effective only in combination with—not in lieu of—instructional improvements during the school day. It is easy to achieve consensus on solutions that do not require teachers to make changes in their day-to-day practice, even when data show that such practices are consistently ineffective. As a school leader, when it comes time to choose a solution from your brainstormed list, you may need to remind teachers that the goal is a solution that changes how students learn in their classrooms. You may find that the more involved teachers are in choosing solutions, the more committed they will be to doing the hard work of implementing them.

A final component of choosing an instructional strategy is for school leaders to determine how much change to take on in the action plan. While some schools will not take on enough—like schools that decide an afterschool program will solve all their problems—most schools that have pursued the improvement process to this point actually take on too much in their action plans. While such enthusiasm is laudable, it is also dangerous. We have seen too many schools come up with a fine list of strategies in their action plan and then not implement any of them well because they are stretching their resources too thin and pushing beyond teachers' capacity to learn and apply new instructional approaches. Under these conditions, most teachers ultimately retreat to their previous practices, which the data showed were not achieving the desired student learning outcomes. School leaders need to be sure not only that the strategies they select are focused on day-to-day instruction in classrooms and are likely to solve the problem of practice, but also that these strategies can be reasonably implemented in the action plan's time frame. Listening to both the "we can do it all" teachers (who are always easier to listen to) and the "we can't do this" teachers (who are always more tempting to ignore) is important in gauging what strategies will effectively and manageably accomplish important changes in practice.

AGREE ON WHAT YOUR PLAN WILL LOOK LIKE IN CLASSROOMS

Anita was concerned. After talking informally with a number of third- and fourth-grade teachers, she began to realize that although teachers had expressed a lot of enthusiasm for using Think Alouds in their reading instruction, each individual seemed to have his or her own concept of what this would actually look like in the classroom.

How your team defines an instructional strategy to address weaknesses in students' skills is a critical part of implementing that strategy. A faculty gains much of its understanding about what the strategy is and why it is the focus of the action plan in the process of selecting the strategy. However, even if your team is faced with the challenge of implementing an instructional strategy that was determined unilaterally (perhaps by district mandate), your faculty can still deepen their understanding and appreciation of the strategy by participating in a discussion of what it actually looks like in practice. We have found that it is important for faculty discussions on this topic to accomplish two particular things: to develop a common vision for implementing the strategy, and to lay out a theory of how the strategy will affect learning.

DEVELOP A COMMON VISION FOR IMPLEMENTATION

It is often not enough to select an instructional strategy by name because it is too easy for people to attach different meanings to commonly used names or words. For example, if you select a strategy that calls for peer editing of draft writing assignments, teachers may have a variety of ideas about what this means. After deciding on an improvement strategy, successful teams develop a shared understanding of what effective instruction looks like by establishing implementation indicators. Implementation indicators include descriptions of what teachers will be doing, what students will be doing, and what the classroom environment will look like when the instructional strategy is in place. The process of creating these indicators allows teams to develop the capacity to have increasingly specific instructional conversations. It also facilitates implementation by making the team's expectations clear. After two team meetings at the Clark School, the third- and fourth-grade teachers produced the following list of implementation indicators for their Think Aloud strategy, shown in Exhibit 6.3:

Exhibit 6.3

IMPLEMENTATION INDICATORS	
CLARK K-8 SCHOOL **Implementing Think Alouds about Inferring:** **What We Will See in Classrooms**	
Teachers	• Model inferring by walking students through their own thought processes as they read a piece of text • Use overhead projectors to display and mark up text while thinking aloud about inferring • Conference with students, asking them to Think Aloud" while reading • Move throughout room to monitor students' inferring
Students	• Know what the word "infer" means and use it accurately to describe their reading process • Use "think aloud" strategies to infer in whole-class, small-group, and conference discussions of text • Answer questions that show their ability to infer
Classrooms	• Display evidence of students inferring from text • Include class-generated poster of what good readers do when they infer for students to reference while reading • Allow flexible arrangement of furniture to enable paired reading, group activities, and sustained independent work
Student Work	• Demonstrates students' ability to infer, predict, connect, and evaluate in their reading journals and other reading assessments

LAY OUT THE THEORY BEHIND YOUR SOLUTION

The Franklin High School math department had invited principal Roger Bolton to join their December meeting. They described with enthusiasm the Problem-Solving Approach and how they planned to implement it across all math classes. "You've got yourself a plan here, and it feels like a good one," said Roger. "Now, can you walk me through how teaching this approach is going to lead our students to become stronger mathematical thinkers?"

Roger's question is deceptively powerful. At this stage in the game, it can be very helpful to push your team to put into words exactly how they believe their plan is going to achieve its desired effect. Chances are, there are a number of ways the plan could produce positive results, and not all teachers agree on the theory behind the solution. For example, do teachers believe that teaching the Problem-Solving Approach will lead to students becoming more independent problem-solvers? Will it increase students' confidence and make them more willing to try problems that they already have the math knowledge to solve but have been too disorganized to tackle? Will it make them pay more attention in math class, thus getting more out of lessons they might ordinarily have tuned out and making them more capable of solving problems themselves? Will it help teachers give students responsibility for deciding what to do rather than relying on teachers to direct them through problems step by step? Alternatively, is the real strength of this strategy that students will be able to use the same approach from class to class and from year to year, thus allowing them to build experience with problem-solving so that it eventually becomes second nature? When pressing teachers to articulate how they think the plan will work, it is also worth asking them if they can imagine any unintended negative consequences. For example, will requiring students to use the Problem-Solving Approach squelch the creativity of real mathematical thinkers by reducing math to following a recipe?[4]

The answers to these questions are not mutually exclusive—in all likelihood, some students will benefit most from consistent instruction from year to year, while others will find it helpful to have a clear strategy for tackling particular assignments. Answering these questions collaboratively will help your team develop a shared understanding of the theory or theories that drive its approach to improving instruction and student learning. Articulating the theory also helps with implementation, as we will see in chapter 8. If teachers understand and agree how the action plan should be addressing the problem of practice, they are more likely to implement the action plan and be able to adapt it to meet students' needs. For example, if the theory behind Franklin's Problem-Solving Approach is that having the process broken into steps will help make it less overwhelming for students so they are more likely to persevere through each step, then a teacher might adapt the steps for her students. If, on the other hand, the theory is that having a consistent strategy from class to class will help students, she should not adapt the steps, but instead make a point of using the exact terminology laid out in the model.

PUT THE PLAN DOWN ON PAPER

Mallory stood up from her desk and took a long stretch. She had offered to convert the scribbles from Franklin High's last math department meeting into a draft action plan for implementing the Problem-Solving Approach. She was amazed at how many steps there were when she typed it all out. Was she making it more complicated than it needed to be?

Exhibit 6.4

DRAFT ACTION PLAN FOR IMPLEMENTING THE PROBLEM-SOLVING APPROACH (PSA)
in Franklin High School Math Classes

OBJECTIVE: To improve multistep problem-solving instruction by teaching a consistent methodology for solving problems in all math classes.

STRATEGY: Teachers will integrate the Problem-Solving Approach into their daily lessons, class assignments, and assessments. Teachers will explain the rubric for evaluating problem-solving to students and will use the rubric regularly in grading assignments.

ASSESSMENT: Students will independently complete two projects, Poster #1 and Poster #2, to demonstrate their ability to apply the Problem-Solving Approach, and a group of teachers will evaluate the posters against a common rubric.

TASK	WHEN
Math department chair and math coach create materials for professional development (PD), including poster rubric and anchor chart listing steps of the problem-solving process to post in the classroom for student reference	January, week 1
Math coach models teaching PSA in four classes; all math teachers attend at least one modeling session	January, week 2
Math coach leads PD session with math department, debriefs model lessons, offers list of poster problems with a range of difficulty	January 18, dept. meeting
Math teachers work in small teams to design PSA lessons for their classes and choose which problems to use for Poster #1 assignment	January, week 3
Math teachers model PSA in classes, share poster rubric with students, and assign Poster #1	January, week 4
Math teachers integrate PSA into regular lessons, students work on posters (Due Feb. 15)	February, weeks 1 and 2
Math teachers work in small teams to assess student work using rubric	February, weeks 3 and 4
Math coach observes four math teachers (volunteers) integrating PSA into teaching and provides over-the-shoulder coaching	February, weeks 3 and 4
Math coach leads PD session with math department, discussing student work and offering guidance for the next round of teaching and Poster #2	March 7, dept. meeting
Math teachers continue to integrate PSA in classes; students work on Poster #2 (Due April 25)	March and April
Math teachers meet weekly in small groups to discuss student work on Poster #2 and other assignments, and administer district math final exams on June 15	May and June

After choosing an instructional strategy and agreeing on what it will look like in practice, it is time to identify the specific tasks that need to be completed for successful implementation. This step involves assigning responsibilities and time frames, as well as planning for how your school will support teachers as they carry out this new work.

Franklin High School's action plan (see Exhibit 6.4) shows one way of summarizing this kind of information, but there are many others. Whatever display you choose, it is important to be very clear about what the tasks are, who is going do them, and when they are going to be accomplished. You will find that your action plan contains two different types of tasks. One type is the instructional strategies that teachers will use in their classrooms when working with students. The other type is professional development activities that are designed to support teachers' implementation of the selected strategy or strategies. Since these two kinds of activity are likely to occur simultaneously, some schools find it easier to capture both kinds of action in a single action plan. Other schools we have worked with prefer to list the activities teachers will be doing in the classroom on a document labeled the "action plan" and the professional development that will support them on a separate document called the "PD plan."

ASSIGN RESPONSIBILITIES AND TIME FRAMES

Writing down what you and your colleagues agree to accomplish and when is an important step in developing internal accountability. This term refers here to what you and your colleagues deem important enough to hold each other responsible for doing. Being specific about responsibilities and committing them to paper creates a shared written history that your school can refer to over time. This document can help teachers think outside their classrooms and consider their larger roles within the school, and can be an important avenue for strengthening and developing shared expectations among teachers, and between teachers, students, parents, and administrators.

When assigning responsibilities and creating a time line for implementation, you'll want to be sensitive to the other demands and duties placed on your teachers, as well as the scope of the plan. The level of detail in the plan will depend on the time frame in which you intend to implement it. If the time line is relatively short, as with the six-month schedule Franklin High adopted, then you may want your action plan to be very specific and indicate what will happen each week. If the time line is longer, like the Clark K-8 School's plan (see Exhibit 6.5), which will be implemented over an entire school year, then the plan may be a bit more broad.

Exhibit 6.5

CLARK THIRD- AND FOURTH-GRADE TEAM READING ACTION PLAN		
Task	Who	When
Find literacy consultant with expertise in Think Aloud strategies and teaching inference	Anita	August-September
Participate in half-day PD with literacy consultant focused on Think Aloud strategies for inferring	Grade 3&4 team members	September-October
Use Think Aloud strategies to demonstrate inferring	Grade 3&4 team members	September-January
Have consultant observe each teacher and provide feedback	Consultant and individual teachers	October-November
Visit each others' classrooms and provide feedback	Grade 3&4 team members	November-December
Participate in half-day PD with literacy consultant focused on common challenges in implementing Think Aloud strategies	Grade 3&4 team members	January
Continue using Think Aloud strategies to demonstrate inferring, refining based on first-semester feedback	Grade 3&4 team members	January-May

If the time line takes you across an upcoming academic year, one option is to prepare an action plan that is more specific for the fall semester and less so for the spring, with the expectation that the spring portion of the plan will be laid out in more detail once implementation is under way and the team can assess its progress. Short-term plans can be helpful for schools that are just beginning the improvement process because they keep the implementation steps concrete, manageable, and immediate. As your school becomes more experienced with using data to improve instruction, you may find that you create action plans designed to be implemented over a number of years.

PLAN HOW TO SUPPORT TEACHERS IN THEIR NEW WORK

What can school leaders do to support the action plan? The first and generally easiest step is to provide the resources teachers need to implement the action plan, which might include books, curriculum materials, chart paper, or overhead projectors. The second and far more challenging step is to help teachers develop the skills and knowledge they need to engage in the heart of the work. The school leaders we know who do the best job of supporting teachers in improving their practice think of themselves as teachers who are working with the other adults in the building as learners.

Support for teachers is most effective if it is coherent, content focused, and frequent.[5] "Coherent" means that the support should align with the action plan; avoid professional development that doesn't directly support the action plan or other schoolwide objectives. "Content focused" means that the support should be specifically grounded in what teachers teach, and may need to provide opportunities for teachers to develop their content knowledge and pedagogy. In one school district we know, elementary teachers took math courses to complement their learning of a new curriculum. The courses were specifically designed to provide the deep level of mathematical knowledge they needed to successfully implement the new curriculum. "Frequent" means that support must be sustained and substantial. Small amounts of time and one-shot workshops will not suffice. Schools we know that are most successful at the work of instructional improvement support teachers at least on a biweekly basis through common planning time or at meetings before and after school. These schools also often dedicate larger blocks of time to significant learning experiences, such as full days during the summer or school year.

Your school culture, which is a reflection of the nature and degree of expectations shared among you and your colleagues, will have implications for how best to provide teacher support and how ambitious you can be in your planning efforts. At the Clark School, where teachers have a strong history of collaborative work, the action plan calls for teachers to regularly observe in each other's classrooms and to offer one another feedback for improving instruction. The same support strategy would probably not work as well at Franklin High, where the math department has a deeply rooted tradition of teacher autonomy and isolation.

Just as strong teachers are expected to differentiate their methods of instruction according to the needs of their students, a thoughtful system of support should account for teachers' different professional needs. How do you know what your faculty needs to be supported most effectively? As with all learners, sometimes it's best just to ask them. We have found that involving teachers in deciding what kinds of support they will be offered goes a long way toward developing the buy-in necessary for successful implementation. One school we know spent two months on extensive plans for the following year's professional development. The instructional leadership team concluded that involving all the teachers in conversations about their professional development needs was critical. The end product was a detailed plan that mapped out how grade-level meetings, content-area meetings, and afterschool sessions would be used together to support teachers.

In sum, developing an action plan is an opportunity to identify relevant and focused professional development for your teachers. Remember, if teachers already had the skills and knowledge they needed to teach differently, they'd probably be doing it. Like all learners, teachers need explicit, specific support in order to improve their practice. Real improvement in student learning takes real time, real resources, and a real commitment to improve. Planning for how to measure whether student learning is in fact improving is the subject of the next chapter.

7

PLANNING TO ASSESS PROGRESS

Jennifer L. Steele and Jane E. King

ANITA, THE TEAM LEADER, DISTRIBUTED THE AGENDA AT THE
Clark School's third- and fourth-grade team meeting. "Are we still planning?" Vivian
said, sounding a bit exasperated. "I thought we finalized the action plan last week.
We're doing Think Alouds, right?" She looked around at her colleagues. "When are
we supposed to take action with our action plan?"

"I'm glad we're all so excited to get started," Anita replied. "But remember that we
haven't yet made a plan for how we're going to measure student progress."

"I think the state and the feds will tell us whether or not we're making progress
all right," Jae replied. "It's called the State Skill Mastery Assessment!"

"To be worth all of the time and energy we are investing," Kristina responded, "this
can't all be just about raising test scores. I didn't become a teacher to spend my days
doing test prep. I mean, I'm trying to help my students become avid readers and critical thinkers. These are complex skills . . . no state test is going to really capture what
my kids can do."

The Clark School is struggling with an essential part of designing a strong action plan:
deciding how to measure progress. Public schools annually confront the question of
how well students are achieving through the state assessments. However, systematically

measuring students' progress isn't an activity that needs to be put on hold until the state test results arrive. Assessing progress is an integral part of the improvement process through which schools increase their internal accountability and find better ways to meet all students' learning needs. Too often, educators begin implementing action plans without thinking about how they will assess progress. As a result, they aren't likely to know whether they're making progress, and they may not even agree on what making progress means in the context of the plan. Schools engaged in improvement work benefit from setting clear goals for student improvement and proficiency, and from deciding in advance how and when they will measure progress toward those goals. This chapter is a guide to developing an assessment plan as part of a school's action plan. Assessment plans address the following questions:

* What assessments will be used to measure progress?
* When will each type of assessment data be collected?
* Who is responsible for collecting and keeping track of the data?
* How will the data be shared among faculty and administrators?
* What are the goals for student improvement and proficiency?

The two most challenging decisions schools confront in developing assessment plans are identifying the kinds of assessments to use to measure progress and deciding how to set appropriate goals for student progress.

CHOOSING ASSESSMENTS TO MEASURE PROGRESS

Just as teachers at the Clark K-8 School and Franklin High School used multiple data sources to explore problems of student performance (see chapter 4), schools should plan to use multiple sources to measure progress in students' learning. We have found it helpful to begin such planning by categorizing the available data sources by three time frames: short term, medium term, and long term. Organizing data sources by time frame encourages the use of multiple data sources and helps make the assessment of progress an ongoing part of the school's professional culture. In general, "short-term data" refers to information that can be collected daily or weekly from students' work and classroom interactions. "Medium-term data" is gathered systematically within a school, grade, or department at periodic intervals during the year. "Long-term data" is gathered annually and includes students' performance on statewide tests. Each type of data can provide important information about what students know and are able to do.

PLANNING TO USE SHORT-TERM DATA

Because short-term data are generated continuously within a school, teachers can use them to make assessments of students' progress a regular, embedded part of their practice. Good sources of short-term data that educators can plan to use to measure progress include students' classwork and homework, classroom observations of student performance, and conferences with students about their learning. In answer to the questions of who will collect the data, when to collect it, and how it will be shared, we've found that responsibility for short-term data collection and analysis is often best delegated to individual classroom teachers because they can examine student work, observe students' participation, and confer with their students on a regular basis. Teachers should keep track of students' learning with some type of formal system, such as spreadsheets or individual student files. Administrators and other teachers can also visit classrooms to collect this kind of data.

Looking at Classwork and Homework

The advantage of using students' classwork and homework to gauge learning is that teachers have access to a constant stream of data. What's more, these data are closely aligned with classroom instruction, so teachers can keep track, in real time, of which students seemed to learn the critical skills of a lesson. Teachers can then use these short-term data to inform their instruction so that it responds to students' learning needs.

In planning to use student work to assess progress, teachers should realize that the task of assessing progress from short-term data goes far beyond checking completion of classwork and homework. The holistic impressions a teacher can glean from skimming the work of an entire class are helpful to a point, but real use of students' work to measure progress entails systematically gathering concrete data. For example, a teacher may prepare a small number of yes-or-no questions that she would like to answer about students' work on a particular assignment. If she has asked students to mark up a short text to show their inferences, these questions might include: Does the student list three or more inferences in the margin of this text? Are at least two of the listed inferences plausible? For an open-response math question, she might ask: Did the student get the question right? Did he begin the question correctly? Did he omit subsequent steps? She could then review each student's work to determine the answers to her questions, which she would record in her grade book or on an electronic spreadsheet where she maintains short-term assessment data.

After collecting the information described above, a teacher should consider its implications for her instruction and look for areas of performance in which groups or individual students continue to struggle. Realistically, teachers would not engage in this level of specific analysis every day. However, the assessment plan should include a strategy for permitting teachers to examine performance in the action plan's priority area (e.g., inferences or multistep problems) at regular intervals.

Schools should consider integrating technological applications into their plans for short-term data collection. For instance, there are now Web-based tutorials for students that can be used to assess students' strengths and weaknesses and provide opportunities for remediation and extra challenge within the classroom. Teachers with access to multifunction copy machines that can read bubble sheets can develop multiple-choice assessments and obtain instantaneous item analyses. One school we know uses a device reminiscent of those used on the TV show *Who Wants to be a Millionaire?* that allows students to indicate their responses to multiple-choice questions displayed on the board. The device records the responses in a format that allows teachers to review not only the distribution of responses but also the responses given by each student. The data generated by each of these applications enable teachers to customize instruction to meet the identified needs of their students as the curriculum unfolds.[1]

One advantage of collecting short-term data is that teachers can bring samples of the data to discuss at meetings of their departments or grade-level teams. The assessment plan should include time for teachers to share and discuss the short-term data they've collected in their classrooms. Ideally, the work teachers share with each other includes direct evidence of the skills that are the focus of the action plan. For instance, each of the math teachers at Franklin High might bring to their department meeting a sample of student work that demonstrates their students' ability to solve multistep mathematics problems. Sharing student work in this manner enables teachers to gain insights from their colleagues about individual students' work, while also encouraging teachers to develop common norms of what high-quality student work should look like.

Observing Students' Participation

Another way schools can plan to measure student learning in the short term is by observing students' participation and demonstrated understanding of a particular concept or skill in the classroom. This kind of observation may be conducted by teachers in their own classrooms or by classroom visitors. Observations can provide rich data on what tasks students are engaged in and how they talk about texts, concepts, and problems they are working on. However, using classroom observations to measure student learning has two limitations. First, it provides more information about the skill levels of the students who participate most vocally than it does about students who are quieter. Second, students may be less willing to take intellectual risks by participating when they are being observed by people other than their teacher. The first limitation is readily addressed by drawing on additional data sources, such as individual conferences or examination of students' written work to develop a more complete picture of student performance. The second limitation can be mitigated by creating a classroom culture in which teachers and administrators frequently observe classes, so that having multiple adults in the room becomes less unusual to students. In our experience, students adjust to observers more readily than teachers do. Talking with students about why visitors are coming can also provide a good opportunity to involve them in discussions about their own learning and the school's efforts to support their learning.

Asking Students about Their Learning

A third and often overlooked strategy for measuring students' progress in the short term is asking the students themselves to talk about their learning. Insights from students can be gleaned through individual conferences, small focus groups, surveys, or written reflections. Conversations can be conducted by teachers in their own classrooms or by colleagues who are visiting classes.

There are several ways to gather information from students about their learning. One approach is to have students share their thinking about a particular academic problem or question while the interviewer takes notes on a conference sheet, as a Franklin High teacher did on a form her team designed (see Exhibit 7.1).

The interviewer can ask students what they're doing, why, and what they're learning. When students talk through problems out loud, it is easy to see where their understanding of a concept is strong and where it falters. This insight can help teachers correct students' misconceptions, either through large-group instruction (when the misconception is common) or through individual instruction (when it is unique to that student).

Another approach to these conversations is to simply ask students to describe how they think about a particular concept in the abstract. For instance, a math teacher at Franklin High School could ask her student what the term "multistep problem" means to him and how he would know when multiple steps are required to solve a problem. She might also ask him about what he learned from particular lessons she had delivered in the past. In situations where classwork and homework show stronger growth for some students than for others, it may be useful to ask students whose learning grew considerably for their thoughts about how they learned the material. At the same time, conversations with struggling learners may provide insights into why these students are not benefiting from the pedagogy embedded in the action plan. The interviewers should share the information gained from these interviews with other teachers so that the faculty can revise the action plan to better meet the needs of all students.

Exhibit 7.1

Franklin High School Individual Student Conference Sheet

Student's Name: Michael Serrano

Date: March 18

Class and Period: Ms. Corning's 4th period Intensive Math

Skill to focus on: Using the Problem-Solving Approach

Teacher's Questions (Summarize what you ask the student to talk about.)	I asked Michael to talk through a word problem in the text that asked him to solve for the rate given the distance and the time.
Student's Responses (Summarize key points in the student's response.)	Michael seemed uncertain and said he would need to know how fast the guy was going. Asked if it was supposed to be in miles. I said, "What do you think?" He stalled, and I asked if there was a formula he might apply. Then a light bulb went on, and he recalled the formula (rate)(time)=(distance). At this point, he plugged in the numbers correctly and solved for the rate.
Student's Understanding (What does the response reveal about the student's understanding of the concept?)	Michael still needs prompting to know when to use a formula he obviously knows how to use. He just doesn't know when to apply the formula. This seems to be a common problem in several conferences I've had with students this week, and it's consistent with the math poster evaluations we did in January.
Implications for Instruction (What does the student's response suggest about future instructional approaches?)	I need to give students more word problems out of context, so they don't rely on the lecture preceding the assignment to determine how to attack the problem. We need to spend more time in class on the "understanding" and "planning" phases of problem-solving, just having kids strategize based on what is given and what is asked for in the problem.

As is the case with all forms of data, having a consistent method for collecting and recording the data from these conversations can support the subsequent analysis because it keeps the data focused and facilitates looking for patterns. In some schools we know, the data team generates and provides teachers with templates for recording information from student conferences; in other schools, grade-level teams, content teams, or the instructional leadership team generates the templates.

As an alternative to interviewing students individually, we also know schools that have conducted focus groups and online surveys of students about their learning. In many cases, these were conducted following a test administration in order to detect areas where students felt well-prepared for the test, as well as areas where they perceived gaps in their own learning. Another useful technique is to ask students to write reflections about their learning on a particular topic. The advantage of focus groups, surveys, and written reflections is that these methods allow teachers to collect information from a large number of students much more rapidly than is possible with individual conferences. The trade-off is that the information may not be as individualized or as detailed as conferences might provide.

PLANNING TO USE MEDIUM-TERM DATA

> Almost from the moment the Franklin math department had agreed that they would all teach a consistent approach to problem-solving, they had been talking about how students could demonstrate their understanding of the approach. Someone had thrown out the idea of asking students to create posters that showed the steps they had taken to solve complex problems, and before they knew it, Poster #1 and Poster #2 had been written into the action plan. Math department chair Mallory Golden liked the poster idea and wanted to make it work. But if they really were going to be able to use the posters to measure student progress, there was still a lot they would need to think through.

Unlike short-term data, which the school generates internally through students' regular work and classroom performance, medium-term data may include both internal and external data sources and is gathered systematically at wider intervals throughout the school year. Medium-term data is helpful for tracking students' progress within a single school year. Sources of medium-term data include commercial tests and locally developed assessments. Some people use the term "formative assessments" to describe tests that teachers give so that they can tailor their instruction to the demonstrated needs of their students. Since these tests are also quite often used (whether they should be or not) for more summative purposes, we prefer the term "benchmark assessments," which captures the idea that the tests help teachers measure how close students have come to mastery of a particular group of skills. The real power in benchmark assessments lies in administering them several times over the year to track students' progress.

Using Benchmark Assessments

Some schools use commercially prepared tests to measure students' performance several times a year. These tests are particularly used in the reading and math content areas and are often in a multiple-choice format. Because some commercial tests provide multiple forms of the test for each grade level, it is possible for a school to administer these tests as many as three or four times a year to gauge students' progress. Many districts decide on the types of medium-term assessments their schools will use and when the assessments will be administered. Schools without such district requirements, however, can choose which tests they want to administer throughout the year.

In selecting a commercial test, as with any assessment, administrators or data-team members must consider the kinds of diagnostic information they want the test to provide. For instance, some measures of student performance yield rich information about the processes students use to complete tasks and are useful in planning instruction. The Formative Assessment of Student Thinking in Reading (FAST-R), used in the Boston Public Schools, is one such instrument. By analyzing the results of this assessment, teachers can learn about the types of errors students make in finding evidence and drawing inferences from texts. When teachers do this kind of analysis together, they can learn a great deal about their students' reading skills. Later, they can confer with individual students about their responses and about where they encountered difficulty, and thus get an even better sense of how to best help students. There are a number of commercial diagnostic reading assessments available.[2] When choosing which assessment to use, it is important to keep in mind the amount of effort needed to administer the assessment (some of the most valuable instruments require teachers to sit with students individually), the speed with which results can be obtained, and the richness of the information they provide.

Using In-House Assessments

"Okay," said Mallory as she opened the December math department meeting. "We agreed we would use a rubric to assess the problem-solving posters. Today we are going to figure out what goes in that rubric."

Adelina said, "How about if we measure how well students complete each of the four steps of the Problem-Solving Approach?"

Will replied, "I think we should start by asking what we want to measure: students' ability to get the right answer, or their ability to use the four-step approach?"

"Well, the PSA is a high-leverage skill that we want them to internalize," said Adelina.

"Um, aren't we then prioritizing the means over the ends?" asked Eddie. "Isn't it most important that they get the question right?"

Developing in-house assessments offers schools tremendous flexibility. Schools can design in-house assessments that are much more specific to what the school is interested in assessing than commercially prepared assessments are likely to be, and they can use these assessments to periodically score students' progress in certain skills. As we see with Franklin High School, when you design an open-ended assessment, you will need to agree on how to score it. Taking the time to develop a common rubric is an important part of this process.

We also know of schools that have developed their own schoolwide quarterly writing assessments and created their own rubrics or adapted widely available writing rubrics like the 6+1 Trait Writing rubric created by the Northwest Regional Educational Laboratory (see Further Reading).

The trade-off in creating internal assessments is that these in-house tests face many of the validity and reliability challenges that were discussed in chapter 2. There are four particular challenges that schools should consider and attempt to address when developing their own assessments. First, each version of the assessment must measure the same skills. If, for instance, Franklin High teachers were to give a permutation problem in January that students could solve through trial and error, and a different permutation problem in March that required students to know the permutation formula, then these assessments would end up measuring largely different skills, probably without the creators intending them to do so. Schools can minimize the risk of this problem by having teachers who are well versed in their content work together to develop the assessment.

Second, difficulty levels should be consistent from one version of the assessment to the next. If a school administers a literary analysis writing prompt using an F. Scott Fitzgerald passage in September and another using a John Milton passage in December, the scores will not necessarily be comparable because there may be a significant difference in difficulty between the two passages. Again, schools can minimize this problem by developing all prompts in advance and carefully considering the difficulty of each. When schools borrow questions from released versions of standardized tests, they may be able to obtain difficulty ratings for each question. Schools can then use these ratings to ensure that assessments are of comparable difficulty from one version to the next.

Third, tests must be administered under standardized conditions. If Franklin High teachers instructed students explicitly to use the Problem-Solving Approach on a January test administration, but left the students to solve the problem in whatever manner they wanted on a May test administration, the scores would not necessarily be comparable. Similarly, if some teachers allowed students to converse during the poster assessments and others did not, the scores would not be comparable between classrooms. Faculty can minimize these problems by deciding collectively on test-administration procedures.

Exhibit 7.2

FRANKLIN HIGH SCHOOL'S PROBLEM-SOLVING POSTER EVALUATION RUBRIC					
	Level 1: Needs Improvement (1 point)	Level 2: Approaches Standard (2 points)	Level 3: Meets Standard (3 points)	Level 4: Exceeds Standard (4 points)	Overall Score for Each Step
Step 1: Understanding	Student does not correctly state what is given or what is asked in the problem.	Student correctly states what is given or what is asked, but not both.	Student correctly states what is given and what is asked in the problem with up to one minor omission.	Student correctly states what is given and asked in the problem with no errors or omissions.	
Step 2: Planning	Student does not accurately list the steps that can be taken to solve the problem. Student does not accurately list information needed to solve the problem.	Student creates a list of information needed to solve the problem, but with some errors or omissions. Student correctly lists the steps that can be taken to solve the problem, but with some errors or omissions.	Student correctly creates a list of information needed to solve the problem with up to one minor omission. Student correctly lists the steps that can be taken to solve the problem with up to one minor omission.	Student correctly creates a list of information needed to solve the problem with no errors or omissions. Student correctly lists the steps that can be taken to solve the problem with no errors or omissions.	
Step 3: Solving	Student does not attempt to solve the problem or attempts to solve it but makes considerable errors.	Student solves part of the question correctly but makes errors in some portions.	Student correctly obtains an answer, but certain steps in the solution are not clear.	Student clearly and correctly solves each portion of the problem.	
Step 4: Checking	Student does not label the units of the final answer. Student does not indicate that the work was checked.	Student labels the units of the final answer, but with errors. Student writes a sentence about checking the work, but does not state how it was checked.	Student correctly labels the units of the final answer. Student writes a sentence correctly indicating how the work was checked.	Student neatly indicates and labels the answer to each step of the problem and the final answer. Student clearly explains not only how the work was checked but also why the answer is reasonable.	

OVERALL SCORE FOR POSTER:_____

Fourth, a consistent scoring system must be established. If teachers are left to use rubrics in whatever way they see fit when they assess students' math posters, essays, or other work, their scores will not necessarily be comparable. One way to minimize subjectivity is by randomly assigning anonymous student assessments to teachers for grading. Schools can also minimize variations in scoring approaches by training teachers to calibrate their scoring as a group. In addition, the school can have two teachers score each assessment, and if the two differ considerably in their scoring, a third scorer can help resolve the disagreement.

As with all assessments, schools should do their best to address these concerns and should not rely too heavily on any single measure. Because medium-term assessments allow teachers to track students over the course of a year, they offer an excellent opportunity for teachers to monitor how individuals are progressing and diagnose what each individual student needs. In addition, these data are valuable for identifying patterns by class, grade level, or other categories.

PLANNING TO USE LONG-TERM DATA

Long-term data, which are data collected on an annual basis, such as statewide assessments, present both challenges and opportunities. Long-term data are often generated by an external accountability system connected to state and federal mandates that relies solely on statewide tests to measure whether schools are meeting the needs of all students. As a result, long-term data are the data that seem to "count" and that schools are under the most pressure to improve. While these pressures can create an important urgency for improvement, they can unfortunately lead schools to adopt a tunnel-vision focus on long-term data as the sole measure of success. Like any single measure of performance, long-term data give one slice of information that needs to be compared with other data to create a complete picture. The following assessment plan developed by the Clark School shows how multiple measures of student performance can be incorporated into an assessment plan (see Exhibit 7.3).

Long-term data can be very helpful for evaluating progress over a longer time frame, such as several years. When the state test remains consistent and the school's scores are averaged over multiple years and compared over time, end-of-year test data can reveal useful information about a school's performance trajectory. While statewide tests may also be used longitudinally to track the performance of individual students from one year to the next, their usefulness for that purpose depends on the forms being comparable across grade levels. Such tests are generally more valuable for examining trends over time than for focusing on individual performance. State tests are also limited in their diagnostic usefulness because in many (but not all) states, the results arrive in the school year after the test is administered.

Exhibit 7.3

CLARK K-8 SCHOOL PROGRESS ASSESSMENT PLAN, THIRD- AND FOURTH-GRADE TEAM					
Data Type	**Measurement Tasks**	**People**	**Schedule for Gathering Information**	**Schedule for Sharing and Interpreting Information**	**Goals**
Short-term data	1. Conduct 1:1 conferences with students in which they draw inferences about written passages.	Grade 3 and 4 classroom teachers	Teachers will confer with five students per week during Sustained Silent Reading and keep records on conference sheets.	Teachers share key findings at one grade-level team meeting in October, December, February, and April.	
Short-term data	2. Observe text-based discussions in grade 3 and 4 classrooms.	Principal Sandy Jenkins Asst. Principal/ Data Manager Bob Walker	Conduct student-focused observations in November and March.	Discuss post-observation findings with teachers immediately after the lesson. Present larger observations about students' inference skills at whole-faculty meetings in early December and early April.	
Medium-term data	3. Assess inferring skills using the district's reading assessment.	Asst. Principal/ Data Manager Bob Walker	Administer the test to all students in the second weeks of September, December, and April. In the first weeks of October, January, and May, data manager receives scores, sorts them by classroom or advisory teacher in Excel, and e-mails scores to the appropriate teachers. Classroom teachers add scores to their records and examine individual students' progress.	In the first weeks of October, January, and May, data manager creates data displays to present at whole-faculty meetings. He also creates grade-level-specific displays to facilitate discussion at grade-level team meetings.	
Long-term data	4. Use statewide, end-of-year test results to determine whether the school made AYP.	Principal Sandy Jenkins Asst. Principal/ Data Manager Bob Walker	Gather results from prior year's assessment in late September, and e-mail to appropriate teachers. Administer current year's test in the second week of May.	In late September, data manager prepares displays for whole-faculty meeting, led by Principal Jenkins.	

SETTING GOALS

Anita was pleased with the plan that she and her grade-level team at the Clark School had come up with. She liked the way they would be looking at data throughout the year to see how students' reading skills were coming along. The only problem now was that she had included a "Goals" column on the plan, and it was looking pretty empty. How should the team think about setting goals for student learning? It seemed like any target they would come up with would be, in some sense, arbitrary. What amount of progress was reasonable to expect?

It is important to establish short-term, medium-term, and long-term goals so teachers have targets to aim for and benchmarks by which to assess their students' progress. Setting goals is part of establishing a culture of internal accountability and high expectations, and of envisioning what's possible. While you may not initially know what constitutes reasonable goals, it's nonetheless critical to set them in order to begin the conversation about how much progress is acceptable and what amount of progress is not. Goal-setting is a recursive process that becomes more precise as schools learn more about their students' learning trajectories.

Goals also need to be sensitive to the improvement process, which is not a steady climb to the summit of schoolwide excellence. School improvement takes a long time and proceeds in dips, plateaus, and surges as teachers learn new skills and incorporate them into their practice. Schools sometimes even see declines in student performance at the beginning of the improvement process because teachers are struggling to master unfamiliar strategies. Schools should be modest, but not pessimistic, in setting their initial goals. However, these goals should become more ambitious over time. As teachers become more confident in using new instructional strategies, and as students internalize teachers' heightened expectations, bolder targets are likely to be warranted.

IMPROVEMENT GOALS AND PROFICIENCY GOALS

When you set progress goals for short-term, medium-term, and long-term assessments, you should establish goals for both improvement and proficiency. This is the same approach some states have adopted in measuring adequate yearly progress (AYP). An improvement goal is a target for students' growth on a given assessment within a specified period of time. One example of an improvement goal would be a one-grade-level rise in the school's average tenth-grade score on a district mathematics assessment between September and May.

By contrast, a proficiency goal is a target for how many students will achieve a level of performance that is considered reasonable and appropriate for students in their grade within a specified period of time. Proficiency goals are not used to measure growth so much as to measure the number of students who have met the performance benchmark. An example of a proficiency goal would be that 70 percent of a school's tenth graders would perform at or above grade level on a district math assessment by the end of the school year.

Establishing both improvement and proficiency goals keeps schools focused on two distinct and important objectives—growth and competence. A school that is pursuing an improvement goal must concentrate on advancing the learning of all students, even those who are currently far below proficient or considerably above proficient. We have worked with schools where most or all of the students are meeting the proficiency mark, but few students are improving markedly. In these schools, improvement goals can be the more relevant measure and a more meaningful motivator for change. However, we've also worked with a school that managed to improve the performance of a large number of students from reading three or more grades below level to reading only one grade below level. This school met its improvement goal because a large number of its students significantly raised their reading scores. However, these students' progress did not help the school meet its proficiency goal because the students remained below the appropriate level for their grade.

Both growth and competence are important for students' real-world success. If students are to be ready to compete in today's economy, it is not enough for their academic performance to show improvement over time. They need to be proficient in problem-solving and communication, among other skills. For students whose performance is less than proficient in either area, improvement isn't enough. Schools must insist on educating all of their students for proficiency, and that means regularly setting progress goals for both proficiency and improvement.

Though states' AYP targets for both improvement and proficiency are based on statewide end-of-year test results, a school's own improvement and proficiency goals need not be limited to end-of-year assessments. Such goals can be established for medium-term assessments as well. The advantage of setting goals with medium-term data is that teachers can measure progress during the school year and adjust their instruction accordingly.

In addition to setting aggregate improvement goals, some schools find it useful to set improvement targets for individual students throughout the year. Setting individual student goals can focus teachers', students', and even parents' attention on what needs to be accomplished. As an example, No Child Left Behind (NCLB) requires schools to develop and implement individual student success plans for each student who performs below the proficient level on state tests. We know schools that design individual learning plans with targets and action steps for all students, as well as schools that take a less time-intensive approach of simply setting goals for each student. In schools that involve students and parents in conversations about goal-setting, students often surprise teachers by setting goals for themselves that are higher than what the teachers would have set for them.

SETTING APPROPRIATE IMPROVEMENT AND PROFICIENCY GOALS

When the Franklin math department began deliberating about target scores on their poster assessment, they ran into a problem. "It seems like we're shooting in the dark here," said one geometry teacher. "I mean, we've never given this assessment before, so we have no idea how kids are going to do on it. We could sit here and say we want to have 100 percent of the students exceeding expectations by the end of the year, but that's just talk. I don't see how we can set goals for performance on this assessment until we have some kind of a baseline for where we are now. Without that, what's the point?"

Setting realistic and appropriate goals involves first analyzing baseline data to determine where your school currently stands and thinking about what long-term success would look like. The next step is to decide how long it should take to move from the current performance level to a level that would constitute success. With this time frame in mind, you can set intermediate goals that will gradually lead to meeting that long-term success target. Under NCLB, states set their AYP goals based on the annual progress necessary for all students to pass their statewide assessments by the year 2014. Individual schools should use a similar process, which means they need to define a long-term goal (such as getting all students to proficiency in reading and math) and then define short-term and medium-term targets that will put them on track to reach that goal within a reasonable amount of time.

As an example, the Clark School currently has 77.7 percent of students reading at grade level. If its long-term, five-year proficiency goal is to raise this mark to 97.7 percent, the school could set intermediate proficiency goals that increase by four percentage points per year. In that case, one medium-term goal would be to have 81.7 percent of students reading at grade level at the end of the next school year. On the other hand, the Clark School might set more modest initial goals, such as a two-percentage-point increase in the first year, followed by more ambitious goals in subsequent years. This would give teachers time in the first year to master new strategies, like Think Alouds, that are part of their action plan. The Clark School might also decide to set an improvement goal, such as an average improvement of three scale-score points at each grade level.

We have seen schools that use other schools as a benchmark by which to set their goals. Sometimes schools look to other schools that are having more success with similar student populations for an idea of what they should aim to achieve. We have also seen schools look to schools with different student populations (for example, urban schools looking at suburban schools) for the same purpose. This approach of looking externally for benchmarks can minimize the potential to underestimate the level of achievement that is possible based on current data.

THE GOLDILOCKS PROBLEM

Just as Goldilocks found herself trying out beds that were too hard and too soft before settling into one that was just right, schools face the difficulty of setting goals that are neither so hard that faculty become demoralized nor so soft that there is little to strive for. It's useful for teachers to set ambitious goals so they are constantly pushing themselves and each other to improve their practice and promote student learning. However, because the improvement process involves ongoing inquiry and learning, schools must keep in mind that progress goals are a means to an end rather than an end in themselves. In other words, missing a lofty target does not necessarily mean complete failure, just as attaining a very conservative goal does not necessarily mean you have achieved raging success.

Setting goals offers schools the opportunity to discuss the big picture of what matters to them—like helping students become learners and thinkers, readers and problem-solvers, and kind and contributing citizens. Setting goals also offers schools the opportunity to establish high expectations for what students can achieve with the support of teachers. Goals that are set internally are merely benchmarks for measuring progress, keeping faculty members focused, and holding ourselves accountable, and they should be seen as such. Attaching extraordinarily high stakes to these goals creates incentives to game the system, as explained in chapter 2. Thus, schools should strive to set ambitious but achievable goals, and maintain the perspective that what matters most is not meeting a particular target but constantly self-assessing to determine what is working and what can be done better to meet all students' learning needs. The following exhibit from Franklin High School shows how goals can be included in an assessment plan. After deciding how, when, and by what standard students' progress will be measured, you are ready to begin implementing your action and assessment plans.

Exhibit 7.4

FRANKLIN HIGH SCHOOL MATH DEPARTMENT PROGRESS ASSESSMENT PLAN					
MONTH	**ASSESSMENT**	**WHO COLLECTS DATA?**	**WHO SHARES DATA?**	**HOW ARE DATA SHARED?**	**PROGRESS GOALS**
Ongoing	Weekly examination of students' responses to open-response classroom assignments	Math teachers	Math teachers	Small groups—final math department meeting of each month	
January	Open-response mathematics poster assessment (baseline)	Math teachers	Dept. Chair Mallory Golden	Math department meetings	35% of students met or exceeded the standard (baseline).
February					
March	Open-response mathematics poster assessment #1	Math teachers	Dept. Chair Mallory Golden	Math department meetings	50% of students will meet or exceed the standard.
April					
May	Open-response mathematics poster assessment #2	Math teachers	Dept. Chair Mallory Golden	Math department meetings	65% of students will meet or exceed the standard.
June	End-of-year state test	Principal Roger Bolton and administrative staff	Principal Roger Bolton and data team	Data team will create graphical displays and present data when results arrive in September of next year.	Average scaled score in math will improve 3 points or more. 40% of students will meet the proficiency level in math.
July	Discussion of progress (reflection on assessment)	Principal Roger Bolton and Math Coach Sasha Chang	Principal Roger Bolton and Math Coach Sasha Chang	Final math department meeting	

8

ACTING
AND ASSESSING

Liane Moody, Mary Russo, and Jonna Sullivan Casey

THE BACK-TO-SCHOOL BUZZ WAS UNMISTAKABLE. THE CLARK K-8 School principal Sandy Jenkins welcomed many returning teachers and a few new ones as she opened the first faculty meeting of the year. "What I'm passing out is a one-page summary of the instructional strategies we developed last spring to improve students' skill at making inferences in a variety of literary genres," she explained. "Since we spent a lot of our time working in grade-level teams, I thought it would be helpful for us all to see how our work in developing student reading skills connects across the school and gets built from grade level to grade level."

On paper, the summary of the action plans for each team made a lot of sense. Yet Sandy had a nagging feeling that bringing these plans to life was going to be a lot harder than anyone expected. What if the focus on the action plan distracted teachers from all the other important things they needed to do? What if teachers struggled with the strategies and gave up quickly? What if teachers didn't implement them with skill and consistency? And, worst of all, what if the strategies didn't make a difference for student learning?

When teachers have worked collaboratively to develop an action plan for improving instruction, you may find that they have a great deal of momentum behind their ideas for change. Actively engaging in the improvement process can empower teachers, inspiring in them the confidence that they play the critical role in improving student achievement and the commitment to fulfill this role to the best of their abilities. Nevertheless, you may find that when it comes time to implement the action plan, your faculty needs you more than ever. Teachers will be center stage as they begin implementing instructional improvements in their classrooms, and will look to you to orchestrate a smooth flow among the various components of the plan and help them regroup when the going gets tough.

The reality of school improvement work is that even with the best planning, when you begin implementation you will inevitably encounter surprises and challenges. Instructional strategies will look different in practice than they did on paper. Students will respond in different ways. As teachers develop more sophisticated knowledge about their practice, new and more complex problems of student learning will emerge. Thus far in the improvement cycle you have been guiding your faculty in an inquiry process; implementation is simply the next logical step in training teachers to look deeply at problems of student learning and develop a disciplined way to respond to them. To capture this spirit, some school leaders describe the action plan as an experiment, a form of action research in which a school tests its theories of how instructional strategies lead to student learning.

Your school teams worked hard to put their action plan ideas down on paper. Now that it is time to bring the ideas up off the paper, four questions can guide your work as a school leader:

* Are we all on the same page?
* Are we doing what we said we'd do?
* Are our students learning more?
* Where do we go from here?

ARE WE ALL ON THE SAME PAGE?

While you may wish teachers could put all of their energies into implementing the action plan, the reality is that any plan for instructional improvement will need to occur in the context of your school's ongoing work. For example, the Clark School's new focus on using Think Alouds with third- and fourth-grade students must occur alongside their district's requirement that all schools implement workshop-style instruction. At Franklin High School, teachers will need to integrate the new problem-solving strategy they've developed with a very explicit and detailed pacing guide for the math curriculum. To help teachers bring the action plan alive, school leaders need to communicate the action plan clearly, integrate the action plan into the ongoing work of the school, and use teams for support and internal accountability.

COMMUNICATE THE ACTION PLAN CLEARLY

How would you like to lead a school where teachers are so focused on student learning that a visitor could ask any one of them about your school's instructional goals and get the same thoughtful answer? Communication prior to and during implementation can help ensure that the goals and strategies of the action plan are well understood and that expectations for teachers and students are clear and consistent across classrooms.

One effective means of communication is the creative use of school documents. While the action plan document itself may comprehensively lay out the step-by-step process teachers will follow to implement an instructional strategy, that document is most likely not the best way to communicate the plan to faculty and staff who were not actively involved in drafting it. Offering instead a one-page summary that sets out the key components of school improvement work can be an important step in helping create an environment in which all teachers are able to describe in specific and concrete language how the school is working to improve student performance. A document that distills the important points from a school action plan, like the Clark School Improvement Plan At-a-Glance shown in Exhibit 8.1, can be effectively shared with everyone in the school community, including students and parents.

At Franklin High, the entire math department was involved in the process of identifying problem-solving as a major student weakness and in identifying the Problem-Solving Approach as a promising way to deal with it. However, not all math teachers participated in every step of putting the action plan on paper. Franklin experienced a common problem of communication that arises when schools attempt to move from having a representative team develop an action plan to having a broader group implement it. To deal with this problem, the math department chair worked to bring all faculty on board by making sure that all math teachers understood the goals for student work, the changes in practice designed to help achieve these goals, and how progress toward these goals would be measured. Communicating this information in a large school building is an important and ongoing challenge.

Exhibit 8.1

THE CLARK K-8 SCHOOL IMPROVEMENT PLAN AT-A-GLANCE			
Standards-Based Student Learning Objective: When information is not explicitly stated in text, students can make carefully reasoned inferences to figure out meaning by combining information in the text with prior experience.			
INSTRUCTIONAL STRATEGIES*			
GRADES 1 and 2	**GRADES 3 and 4**	**GRADES 5 and 6**	**GRADES 7 and 8**
Use oral questions after Read Alouds to push discussion from facts to higher levels of meaning—e.g., What made you say that? How did you know that? Demonstrate and require students to justify or "prove" their answers orally with new information learned.	Continue oral questions and proving your answer techniques from Grades 1 and 2, applied to more challenging pieces of writing. Model Think Aloud process for using information from text to back up conclusions and opinions both orally and in writing. Provide students with questions in written format for reference when practicing Think Alouds.	Continue oral questions, proving your answer, and Think Aloud techniques from prior grades, applied to more challenging pieces of writing. Model use of two-column format in Reader's Response notebooks to ask, record, and answer questions about text that require reading between the lines (inferring). In Literature Circles, one-to-one teacher conferences, class discussions, and writing assignments, require students to back up opinions with solid reasons that are both stated and implied in text.	Continue oral questions, proving your answer, Think Aloud, Reader's Response notebooks, and discussion techniques from prior grades applied to more challenging pieces of writing. Apply all of above techniques to character analysis in literary genres required at Grades 7 and 8—e.g., How is the character developed and revealed through what he/she says? What others say about him/her? What he/she does?

*Use of these instructional strategies includes providing students with exposure, modeling, shared practice, guided practice, and independent work to ensure these strategies are taught, demonstrated, practiced, and applied.

ASSESSING PROGRESS		
SHORT TERM	**MEDIUM TERM**	**LONG TERM**
Observations of discussions in classrooms for each grade; students selected at random can give detailed examples and explanations for opinions.	Student responses on items testing inference skills using district's formative reading assessments (Sept./January/June) show increase in correct responses.	Pattern of student responses on items testing inference skills on statewide, end-of-year tests shows increase in number of correct responses.

INTEGRATE THE ACTION PLAN INTO ONGOING SCHOOL WORK

Being clear about what the action plan entails is an important task. But it can be equally important to make sure that your school's other instructional goals are not eclipsed by the new plan. A good way to do this can be to work with your faculty to develop a school-wide curriculum map and describe how your new strategies fit into this overall plan.

At the Clark School, principal Sandy Jenkins and her leadership team had created a schoolwide English language arts curriculum map based on the state curriculum frameworks, district guidelines, and their own action planning. For each English language arts state learning standard, the team compared what each grade level would be covering each week of the school year to ensure that teachers would teach all standards to all students over the course of a year. Anyone who consulted this map, which was prominently displayed outside of the school office and posted in individual classrooms, could see what topics would be featured when at each grade level. The map proved extremely helpful when grade-level teams met to figure out how to integrate the instructional strategies from their action plans into their ongoing work.

USE TEAMS FOR SUPPORT AND INTERNAL ACCOUNTABILITY

As he looked around at the department meeting, principal Roger Bolton could see that Anne McGovern and Jean Louis felt lost. As teachers of "intensive math" at Franklin High School, their classes were filled with the weakest math students in the building. Both new teachers, they were pleased to be included in the math department's process for analyzing data and brainstorming instructional improvements. They were enthusiastic about the Problem-Solving Approach that the department had chosen. But now that it was time to actually start teaching it, the plan seemed out of reach. "I don't see how we can teach this method," Roger heard Jean mutter at the end of the meeting "if our students can't actually read the problems we give them or do the most basic calculations that they ask for."

When you first began organizing for collaborative data analysis, as a school leader you worked to build a system of interlocking teacher teams. Now that it is time to implement your action plan, these teams can become an important source of support and inspiration for teachers. As teachers become accustomed to checking in with their colleagues regularly, they make a greater effort to be prepared for meetings. As teachers see their teammates working hard to implement the strategies, they are motivated to do their best to make changes in their own classrooms. And as teachers realize that they eventually will be turning over their students to the next year's teachers—who will expect students to have experienced the teaching practices agreed on in the action plan—they develop an increased sense of personal responsibility for their students' performance. After all, no one wants to leave her colleagues in the lurch (or be embarrassed that she is not up to snuff).

There may be times, however, when you discover that the team structures you put in place are not enough, and that you may need to facilitate the development of new collaborations. Principal Roger Bolton guessed that one of the reasons intensive math teachers were frustrated was that they needed guidance about how to make the Problem-Solving Approach more accessible to their students. So Roger arranged to have the math department meet with English as a Second Language specialists and special education teachers to discuss how to provide more instructional supports to scaffold student learning, such as breaking the steps of the approach into smaller units that could be taught over a longer period of time. Because Roger had involved all faculty in exploring math performance at the beginning of the year and then later shared the math department's action plan with the whole school, all teachers were quite familiar with the task at hand. Encouraging faculty to work across disciplines to figure out how to connect the instructional goals of the school to their daily lessons can be a powerful way of making sure implementation gets off the ground, especially when considering the learning of at-risk or struggling students.

ARE WE DOING WHAT WE SAID WE'D DO?

As a school leader you can begin to keep track of how things are going almost from the moment teachers start implementing the action plan. Monitoring is critical to ensure a smooth launch and to clearly signal to teachers that this work is so important to you as the school leader that you intend to give it your personal attention. There is no point in waiting until the implementation period is well underway to get a read on whether teachers really integrated the instructional strategies into their practice. If you wait that long and then find out that things did not go well, it's like looking into a rear-view mirror—the action is past, and it is often too late to change it. If you stay involved from the beginning, you can become a helpful partner in making sure that instruction really changes. To do this, you may find it helpful to visit classrooms frequently, promote consistency rather than conformity in instructional practices, and adapt professional development plans to meet ongoing needs that emerge from the work.

VISIT CLASSROOMS FREQUENTLY

Our experience in schools is that classroom visits are an indispensable part of supporting teachers in improving their instruction. As part of the process of learning to examine instruction (discussed in chapter 5), your school may begin to develop a culture in which classroom visits from colleagues are a comfortable part of school life, and you may find that this culture deepens during the implementation phase. There are a variety of protocols that you can use to increase the chances that classroom visits will be productive. We have had particular success with LearningWalk, developed by the Institute for Learning,[1] and many schools have developed classroom visit guides of their own.[2]

The basic idea behind visiting classrooms is that the best way to understand what is happening instructionally is to actually see it for yourself. Effective classroom visit protocols have several things in common. The purpose is to support teachers in improving the very heart of their instructional practice, not to evaluate them for job performance or other reasons. The focus is on observing what teachers do—in the way they set up their classrooms, interact with students, and assign work—to help students learn, and on observing whether students are in fact learning. The participants can include the principal or other teaching colleagues. To be most effective, the protocol involves participants using materials that consist of guiding questions or worksheets that help ensure that participants know what to look for and collect evidence that can later be discussed, analyzed, and used for reflection. Exhibit 8.2 shows Mallory's notes after visiting a tenth-grade geometry class.

There are three key ingredients for successful classroom visits. One is ensuring that there is a clear focus, such as looking for evidence of the investigative approach to math instruction. Another is that the observers identify ahead of time the specific questions they will try to answer, which could include questions such as "Are students able to explain how they use math materials independently?" and "During classroom discourse, are students explaining their answers and reasoning?" A third key ingredient is that the participants take time after the visit to provide feedback to the teachers observed so that they can raise questions, examine practice, and develop shared insights into improving student learning.

One school we know developed a very detailed protocol for conducting classroom visits. Recognizing that it would be impossible for an individual to observe all aspects of classroom practice at once, the school's protocol involved having four classroom visitors at a time, each charged with making observations about a specific area of practice. Because their action plan focused on improving the use of questioning and conversations in teaching, the four areas of practice targeted by the protocol were looking at what types of questions teachers ask, what kind of evidence there is for conversations

Exhibit 8.2

Franklin High School Classroom Visit Feedback Notes

Please focus your observations on how the Problem-Solving Approach helps students learn to solve multistep math problems. Keep in mind the following focus question:

What evidence do you see that students use the Problem-Solving Approach in their group and independent work?

Try to be as specific as possible about what you saw students doing and how you knew what they were or weren't learning.

Teacher Observed: Anne Marie McGovern   **Class:** Geometry 110B

Date: April 6   **Grade:** 10

What I Saw:

Walls:

Steps of problem-solving approach on board at front of room; difficult to read from back of room

What Students Were Doing to Learn:

Students working in groups of three—very engaged. Problem asked them to use their knowledge about angles to design stage lighting for concert. One student asked, "Should we be using the same steps on the board like we used for the last problem?" Other students told him it was okay, but that he didn't have to use all the steps all the time. In one group, kids seemed confused about what to do. One student raised his hand for help for the group, but the teacher was working with another group. No students in this group wrote anything down on their papers.

Presentations/Exhibits:

Poster assignments displayed all around the room. Student names were on them. Three posters had incomplete and incorrect solutions.

What Was Worthy of Note:

Most students seem to know what the Prob.-Solve App. is and that it has certain steps. Most groups discussed their plan to use it. Some students discussed alternatives, such as drawing each part of the problem.

Questions I Have:

Should math dept produce an enlarged PSA steps chart for display in all classes with individual copies for each student to use for reference?

What steps can teacher take to eliminate confusion with each group during class time?

Should student work with incorrect answers really be on the walls or can students do a rewrite before displaying?

What are the next steps toward having students move toward independent use of PSA?

Observer: Mal Golden

about learning, physical evidence of improvement strategies, and students' perspectives on their work. Each observer was given a note-taking form unique to the area he or she was observing. The entire classroom visit protocol called for a meeting immediately before the visit to give an overview about the tour, two classroom visits of 15 minutes each, and a postmeeting to debrief on the experience.

PROMOTE CONSISTENCY RATHER THAN CONFORMITY

When you visit classrooms, you are bound to find as many variations on the action plan as you have teachers. The challenge for school leaders involves distinguishing between skillful adaptations that move teachers to more sophisticated ways of supporting student learning and unskillful ones that water down or distort the spirit or intent of the original plan.

Clark principal Sandy Jenkins had worked hard to encourage teachers to faithfully implement their action plans. But on one visit to Vivian Muteba's fourth-grade classroom, she began to question the value of her efforts. As Sandy observed the teacher leading the class in a Think Aloud exercise, she could see that two students seemed to hold back from the activity. When the teacher called on one of these students, he was clearly uncomfortable and struggled to put his ideas into words.

When Sandy expressed her concerns to the teacher after the visit, Vivian knew just what she was talking about. "Jeffrey struggles with activities that put pressure on him to speak up," she explained. "But if I don't call on him he just tunes out and misses the lesson. I used to work with Jeffrey and several students with similar difficulties separately to show them how to underline key words that helped them figure out the deeper meaning of what they were reading, but with the focus on whole-class Think Alouds, I stopped doing that."

Sandy is faced with a leadership challenge that arises for many school leaders when they work to change instructional practice: the difficulty of promoting consistency while supporting teacher creativity. In communicating the action plan to teachers, Sandy may have overemphasized the importance of consistency in implementing the action plan without highlighting the equal importance of allowing room for teachers to employ their knowledge and creativity in responding to the needs of diverse learners, particularly struggling learners. Vivian will not be able to truly improve her practice if she strives simply for conformity—faithful implementation of a plan that may wind up leaving behind some of the students who need her individualized insights most.

Striving for consistency involves getting to the deeper "why" behind instructional strategies, just as you did when you first examined instruction (see chapter 5). For the Clark School the goal of the action plan is to use teaching strategies that encourage students to "think about how they think" as a means of developing inference skills in reading, not to make sure all students participate in a particular activity such as Think Alouds. Consistency involves the deeper question: How can we achieve our instructional goals with all students?

Although achieving consistency may be quite difficult, it is a worthwhile goal for several reasons. One is that if you think of the action plan as an experiment, the only way to truly test your hypothesis that your new instructional strategies will improve student learning is to faithfully implement those strategies and then see what happens. Another reason is that in striving for consistency, teachers develop a shared understanding of what constitutes effective instruction, and this understanding is essential in making ongoing improvement part of the everyday work of your school. The most important reason, however, is that students can benefit enormously from consistent instruction. It helps them integrate what they learn as they move from teacher to teacher during the school day or from one grade to the next, and ensures that all students in all classrooms throughout the school have similar opportunities to learn.

Despite the virtues of consistency, it is important to recognize that, given the needs of diverse learners, it is a rare instance when a single strategy or set of strategies will meet the needs of all students. Teachers are perfectly positioned in the classroom to really explore the chosen instructional strategies and try to improve them in the context of solving learning problems. When they report on their adaptations, the whole school can learn what it takes to elevate the learning of all students.

Some examples we've observed of helpful adaptations involved an action plan in which teachers used a math routine called "number of the day." During a 10-minute segment of instructional time, teachers asked students to brainstorm strategies for computing that day's number and then displayed the strategies on large chart paper in the classroom. The theory behind the plan was that if students have regular opportunities to explore numbers in an open-ended way, guided by the teacher and with other students so they build their knowledge in a social context, they will become more comfortable with numbers and develop an intuitive sense of the many ways numbers can be used. Teachers worked with the class to record the ideas their students generated, and the principal reviewed them during her classrooms visits. One first-grade teacher noted that some students in her class were not as forthcoming with their strategies as others. To inspire these children to see that they were capable of generating strategies that were just as good as those of students who spoke up more readily, the teacher decided to designate certain students the day before to be the first to share their ideas the next day for the number of the day task.

Another teacher made a different modification. When he saw that his students were not producing as many math strategies as he would have liked, he decided to leave the 10-minute math chart paper up all day long and let students add strategies during free times throughout the day, such as lunch or recess. The result was a dramatic increase in the number and quality of strategies students generated. In modifying the instructional strategy, these teachers were able to make changes that made it more likely children would experience the heart of the strategy: stress-free exploration as a way to build comfort and confidence in manipulating numbers.

ADAPT PROFESSIONAL DEVELOPMENT PLANS TO MEET ONGOING NEEDS THAT EMERGE FROM THE WORK

Franklin High School math teachers had been using the Problem-Solving Approach in their classes for six weeks. The action plan called for their March professional development session to offer guidance about assigning and grading Poster Assessment #2. As math coach Sasha Chang and department head Mallory Golden met with the principal to plan the session, they began by sharing some concerns.

"I'm not so sure we should focus our professional development on the rubric again," began Sasha. "I've been in a lot of classrooms, and I'll tell you what I'm seeing: teachers are using the Problem-Solving Approach, that's for sure. But it seems like it's kind of taken on a life of its own. Instead of focusing on helping students get good at thinking for themselves, they are focusing on helping them get good at following the steps of the process. Teachers seem to be placing more emphasis on evaluating whether the students follow the steps instead of evaluating the thinking that actually happens at each step."

"My sense is that quite a few teachers realize this is happening," Mallory responded. "I've had a few people come up to me and say that they like the approach, but they feel the training on it just hasn't gone deep enough. They find themselves just walking students through the 'understand' phase of the problem, doing much of the work for the kids themselves because they're just not sure how you teach that part of the process."

When you first created your action plan, you took your best guess at what kinds of professional development your faculty would need to support them in the work. Once you begin implementing it, however, you may find that you have to modify your plans, either by changing the content of scheduled sessions or by adding additional ones to make sure teachers get the help they need. One school we know used a "just-in-time" approach to ensure that teachers were thoroughly prepared to teach each unit of a new math program. They arranged for a workshop to be held just before the teaching of key units at each grade level so that teachers could review the lesson, materials, and teaching moves required immediately before they taught them.

For teachers to make meaningful change in their practice, they may need to make multiple attempts to integrate new ideas. Instead of being discouraged when things do not go perfectly the first time around, as a school leader you can focus your efforts on understanding why teachers are having trouble with certain aspects of your plan. If you structure professional development so it is flexible and provides opportunities for teachers to learn, try out, analyze, get feedback, and reflect on new practices, you can show teachers that you are there to support them during this hard work.

For example, an action plan for improving writing skills might call for the use of one-on-one conferencing with students about their writing. For teachers unfamiliar with this practice, incorporating it meaningfully into their teaching might require that they have an the opportunity to see another skilled teacher demonstrate key components of conferencing, such as asking appropriate questions, giving specific feedback, and guiding students in editing. After that, teachers would most likely need ongoing opportunities to try out this practice in their classrooms and meet with other teachers to discuss, analyze, and reflect on their implementation and the results they were getting. You can demonstrate the depth of your belief in professional development by participating in sessions along with teachers; you model the importance of professional learning by being a learner yourself. In creating and supporting ongoing opportunities for professional development, a school leader reinforces the idea that the goal of school improvement work is to create of a school culture in which everyone is learning.

ARE OUR STUDENTS LEARNING MORE?

Although supporting teachers in improving their practice is an important part of your job during implementation of the action plan, as a school leader your ultimate responsibility is to keep your faculty focused on student learning. After all, the main reason your school developed an action plan was to increase student learning, and the main reason you developed an assessment plan was to be able to measure the extent to which you reach this goal. You can keep the focus on learning in the short term by regularly checking in with teachers about learning outcomes. In the longer term, you can help teachers see the big picture and be honest in evaluating what is working or not working.

REGULARLY CHECK IN WITH TEACHERS ABOUT LEARNING OUTCOMES

Sandy Jenkins had learned a lot by visiting Clark School classrooms throughout the fall to observe how teachers were implementing the strategies outlined in their action plans. As part of her visits, she tried to make a point of looking through student work and talking with the children themselves about what they were learning. A couple of days after the winter results of the district's reading assessment were in, Sandy stopped by third-grade teacher Jae Kim's classroom to have a more concrete discussion about how things were going.

"I noticed that your class made some real progress on the December assessment," Sandy began. "Can you tell me more about what you saw in the data and how it affects the way you will approach the next few months?" Jae showed Sandy a spreadsheet that displayed the results of the district test alongside his own assessment of each student's performance from conferencing notes, then explained to her his findings: "Well, although most students reached or exceeded their targets on the district assessment, you can see that there are three kids who fell pretty far short. For Danny and Keisha, I saw this coming. You can see from my notes that Danny is still at the decoding stage and Keisha just can't seem to get past the literal meaning of the words. As for Marissa, I'm really surprised at her score. If you just sit with her as she reads and talks about a book she's read, she seems to know what's going on. Maybe she has trouble transferring her knowledge into a testing situation? Anyway, I'm a little concerned about how to reach these kids. They all need something different and there just doesn't seem time in the day to give it to them."

In the days before your school was engaged in a process of continuous improvement, it might have been awkward to sit down with a teacher in the middle of the year and ask him what he could tell you about how much his students were learning. But once you have action and assessment plans in place, initiating these kinds of discussions can become much more comfortable. When teachers begin to understand that you are an ally in their struggle to help each child reach his or her potential, you may find that they begin to look forward to these encounters and actively solicit your advice in finding solutions.

Sandy and Jae had their conversation about the performance of struggling learners in his class before it was too late. By the end of their discussion, Sandy had offered to have a literacy specialist work with Jae's neediest students intensively over the next several weeks right in the classroom, so that Jae could see some of her teaching moves and begin to use them himself. She offered to join the next third- and fourth-grade team meeting to participate in their discussion about whether Think Alouds were making a difference for students who were still working to master the most basic reading skills. Another strategy she came up with was to ask the school's parent liaison to make a particular effort to reach out to the families of these three students and make sure that they understood the extra support their children would be getting.

Collecting short-term and medium-term data on student learning in the way described in chapter 7 provides direct and immediate evidence about whether students are learning and gives you an opportunity to make midcourse adjustments in the plan if they aren't. When you focus on what multiple data sources reveal about student learning, you can remain true to the goals of the plan while modifying the instructional approach when needed. Maintaining the ability to change midstream requires treating the action plan as a dynamic document, so that teachers don't see it as a straightjacket but as a living, organic process tailored to the school's needs for improvement and serving the school's mission to focus on instruction.

HELP TEACHERS SEE THE BIG PICTURE

Math department chair Mallory Golden collapsed into the chair in principal Roger Bolton's office and let out a long sigh. "Take a look at this," she said as she handed over a chart showing Franklin High's performance on the most recent state math test. "All that work on the Problem-Solving Approach and the percentage of our students scoring in the lowest two proficiency levels has barely budged. According to the rubrics we've been using, our students have made big strides in tackling multistep problems. How do I tell my teachers that all that hard work was for nothing?"

After leading your school through a difficult process of change, it can be frustrating when you don't see results right away. During his regular visits to classrooms, Roger observed firsthand the visible changes in math instruction at Franklin High that seemed to engage more students in learning. He feels instruction in math is finally on the right track. They still have a long way to go, but he knows it is up to him to make sure that they don't allow a quick look at the data to throw cold water on their efforts.

Helping teachers see the big picture means encouraging them to think about whether they have really explored the data completely and whether they have taken into account the many other indicators of student learning available to them as a school, as well as the many other ways to present data. When Mallory and Roger looked closer at the numbers, they realized that although the percentage of tenth graders scoring in the "Failing" and "Needs Improvement" categories of the test had not changed much since the previous year, more students were now in the higher of these two categories. Students had higher raw scores within each proficiency level than they had in previous years, but because of the way the results were reported, these differences were not readily seen. They also noticed that the percentage of students taking the test was noticeably higher than it had been in previous years. This could mean that some of the weakest students, who traditionally had avoided school and testing days, this year had the confidence to at least give the test a try. By looking at the same data in a more detailed way, they had a more complete picture of the effects of implementing their action plan for math.

Exhibit 8.3

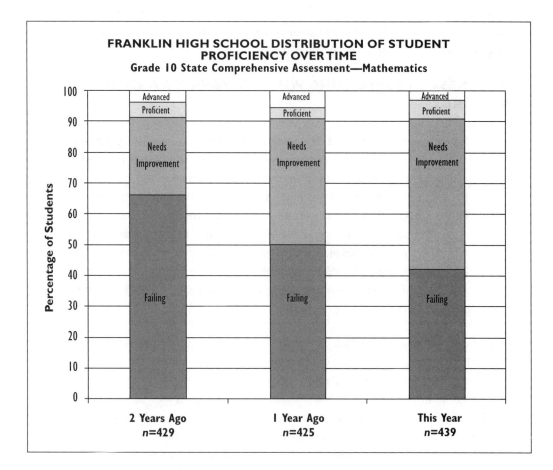

Helping teachers see the big picture also means managing expectations around the question of how soon it is reasonable to expect to see improvements in scores on external tests of accountability. When Roger saw that the math faculty's assessment plan set a target that Franklin High would meet Adequate Yearly Progress goals on the state math test, he let them do it. After all, he reasoned, meeting this target was a measure by which many people would judge the school. Nevertheless, Roger knew that it would take time for teachers to develop skill and competence in teaching the Problem-Solving Approach. Also, the plan had only been in effect for the second half of the school year, and there had been some glitches along the way. This meant that in a number of classrooms students only had a month or two of solid training in the methodology. Given these factors, Roger felt that it was too soon to use the state test results to judge whether the plan was successful or not, so he encouraged his faculty to try the approach for another year. He also shared with teachers his own evidence and observations from his classroom visits that instruction in math classes was improving.

BE HONEST IN EVALUATING WHAT IS WORKING AND NOT WORKING

Sandy carefully reviewed the charts that the data team had prepared showing changes in student reading performance over the last school year. Although all grades had made progress, she noticed an interesting phenomenon: the improvement among the fifth and sixth graders was much stronger than the movement among third and fourth graders. To build each team's commitment to the plan, she'd made the conscious decision to let each grade-level team choose its own instructional strategies for achieving the schoolwide goal of helping students become more skilled readers. But now she wondered: Was there a chance that the strategy adopted by the third- and fourth-grade team was not as effective as the strategy adopted by the fifth- and sixth-grade team?

Sandy faces a delicate situation. The third- and fourth-grade team implemented their Think Aloud strategy with zeal all year. Yet student performance on the district-mandated formative reading test was not that impressive. As a school leader, you may find that once the data come in you need to help your teachers take a hard look at whether the strategies they may have worked so hard to implement really made a difference. This can be difficult, because when people believe strongly in their ideas they often become "pet projects" in which a lot of energy and time is invested, and they may become unwilling to look at signs that those strategies are not working with some or all of their students. While we do not want to encourage schools to simply abandon strategies that do not produce results across the board, it is important to take a careful look when learning outcomes are not as robust as you had hoped. As a school leader, your responsibility will sometimes be to point out when a well-designed and well-executed strategy just isn't doing the job.

Exhibit 8.4

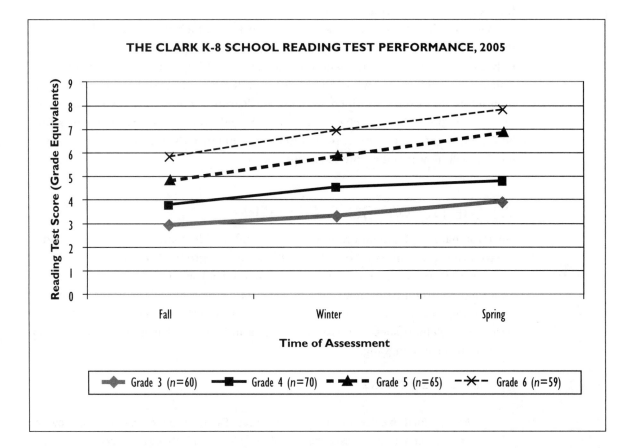

THE CLARK K-8 SCHOOL READING TEST PERFORMANCE, 2005

In the case of the Clark School, the graph of reading test performance would not be enough to tell Sandy whether the third- and fourth-grade strategy was problematic, and certainly would not be enough to tell her why. There are plenty of reasons why the average growth patterns might be different for different grade levels. Sandy would need to consider this graph in combination with other data, such as her observations during her classroom visits that the Think Aloud approach did not seem to work well with certain students, or her observations during classroom visits of the upper grades that might have shown those teachers having particular success with Reader's Response note-books and Literature Circles. When Sandy begins a conversation with her faculty about whether they might need to supplement or replace their chosen strategy, she can raise questions such as Are we truly implementing the strategy to the extent we planned? Have we been doing it long enough? Is it working for all learners? Is this strategy power-ful enough to be our primary focus?

Viewing implementation as an experiment from which the school will learn new things about effective instruction can help school staff approach their own work hon-estly and critically. As you evaluate the effectiveness of implementation (the extent to which we are doing what we said we'd do) as well as the effectiveness of the strategies themselves (the extent to which students are learning more), it helps if you remain open to the possibility that change may be required. In this way you help your school become invested in student learning rather than in any particular strategy. Sometimes the data will show that it is time to change course.

WHERE DO WE GO FROM HERE?

Once you have implemented your action plan and the ideas and practices embodied in it have been tried out with consistency, it is time to regroup. No doubt you and your faculty have learned a lot and probably determined that you have a lot more to learn. It's important to ground the next level of work solidly in evidence of student learning. Three things you can do once you have made it around the steps of the improvement cycle are to celebrate success, revisit your criteria and raise the bar, and plan how to keep the work fresh and ongoing.

CELEBRATE SUCCESS

At the final faculty meeting of the year, Sandy surprised her teachers by not passing out a series of data charts. "We're going to talk about a different kind of data today," Sandy began. "We've worked hard all year to try to improve reading instruc-tion in our school. We've had our ups and our downs, but I think every one of us has learned something. On the paper I am distributing, I'd like you to take a few minutes to describe something in your teaching this year with which you were successful. Be sure to write down evidence of its success and the reasons why you think your effort worked. After you've had a chance to jot down your ideas, evidence, and reasons, we're going to divide into cross-grade groups and use a protocol that allows us to really get at the heart of what success looks like, sounds like, and feels like."

Exhibit 8.5

THE CLARK K-8 SCHOOL TIME LINE FOR COMPLETING THE STEPS OF THE IMPROVEMENT PROCESS

	Step of the Improvement Process							
	Organize for Collaborative Work	Build Assessment Literacy	Create Data Overview	Dig into Data	Examine Instruction	Develop Action Plan	Plan to Assess Progress	Act and Assess
Aug.	■	■	■					
Sept.	■	■	■					
Oct.	■		■	■				
Nov.				■				
Dec.				■	■			
Jan.				■	■			
Feb.				■	■			
Mar.					■			
Apr.					■	■		
May					■	■	■	
June					■	■	■	
July								
Aug.	■		■					
Sept.	■	■	■	■	■			■
Oct.				■	■			■
Nov.				■	■			■
Dec.				■	■			■
Jan.				■	■			■
Feb.				■	■			■
Mar.				■	■			■
Apr.				■	■			■
May				■	■	■	■	■
June				■	■			■

So often teachers are asked to look at test scores or their own practice and talk about what went wrong. We have found that tempering this by giving teachers a chance to think deeply about what makes for successful practice can be a very positive learning experience. Using a formal protocol such as the Success Analysis Protocol Sandy used at the Clark School can help ensure that the conversation gets beyond simple platitudes and continues the practice of talking about teaching in a fine-grained way.[3] Giving teachers a chance to talk together about their own success and reflect on the reasons for that success does more than give them a well-earned moment of appreciation. It also allows them to begin to internalize the qualities at the heart of best practices, such as evidence, analysis, and reflection, and to think about how to bring these qualities more strongly into their work.

Another way to celebrate success involves simply showing your faculty how far they have come. Sandy used the figure shown in Exhibit 8.5 to show her faculty how they had worked through the eight steps of the improvement cycle, often managing a number of different tasks at once, in order to make progress in their work.

There are, of course, many other ways of celebrating success that may rely more heavily on making public the results of your student assessments. Success can be defined collectively or individually, and progress as well as achievement can be acknowledged for both students and teachers. What is important is that a collective sense of accountability for results is built among teachers. Acknowledgments of progress are especially powerful for students when they can be broadly distributed across all student groups, and not just among high achievers who are accustomed to recognition. Since scores on some commercial formative reading assessments are progressive across years, students can be acknowledged for improvement of more than one year's progress. At one middle school awards assembly, students whose district reading assessment scores improved by 100 points or more received certificates. Their names were read along with the improvement made. Students with failing grades, students who frequently get in trouble, and students in separate classes were all greeted with "oohs" and "aahs" when the audience heard that they had improved by 100 points, 200 points, or even more in some cases.

Displays of student work in meeting standards provide another example of how authentic success can be celebrated. The actual work produced by students as they worked to meet standards indicates their progress in striking ways. In one school, each classroom teacher put up a "Wall of Work" in each classroom and the principal created schoolwide displays showing the work of every student in the school. In another school, to reward students' efforts to improve their writing, teachers displayed not just the final pieces of writing, but the brainstorming sheets, outlines, first drafts, and edited drafts as well. They did this in order to show concretely the hard work that it takes to get to standards and to remind students that, with effort, everyone can improve.

REVIST YOUR CRITERIA AND "RAISE THE BAR"

Roger met with the Franklin High math department and talked with them about the disappointing performance of tenth graders on the state math exam. "Let's not let this get us down, folks," he told them. "Some of the posters the kids created, especially for the most recent assignment, are quite impressive. You seem to have hit on a type of assignment that captures their imagination and an approach to tackling word problems that gives kids something to hold on to."

"The second round of posters did go quite well," Mallory added. "In fact, for most steps of our rubric, we met our target of having 75 percent of our students score 'Meets Expectations' or better."

"I wonder," Roger replied, "whether it's time to take another look at that rubric and the way we apply it. Let's be sure that when we say a piece of work 'Meets Expectations' we are talking about high expectations. When we first got into this problem-solving thing we weren't quite sure what it was reasonable to ask of kids. Now that we've seen a little of what they can do, I think we can start asking for more. How about taking a look at the scoring rubric used in the state exam? We want to be sure there is alignment between how we assess students and how the state does."

As teachers gain understanding of the strategies they are implementing, as a school leader, you can help them adjust the criteria by which success is measured to promote the deeper understanding of the material that comes once they have been implementing for a while. By revisiting the conversations they had when they were first developing shared understandings and expectations for the work, teachers can begin to redefine what is possible. At Franklin, teachers had very little experience using a systematic approach to evaluate students' demonstrations of their problem-solving strategies. At first, they may have made their rubric too easy or made their grading too lenient. By sticking with the strategies and refining them, they can collectively come to better and more nuanced understandings of what good work really looks like.

For a school that is implementing a new set of instructional techniques, very visible signs of implementation—like the prominent display of student work—may be one way of demonstrating success. For a school in which teachers are refining their practice, the criteria will need to become more refined and more focused on complex teaching and learning skills. For example, more refined criteria could include that the student work displayed shows evidence of students' reasoning and students' use of a rubric to critique their own work. As the criteria change, the ongoing feedback teachers receive from the principal evolves to push their practice toward higher goals. By continuing the conversations in which teachers reflect on their practice and their goals for student learning, the criteria for success will continue to deepen along with teacher learning.

PLAN HOW TO KEEP THE WORK FRESH AND ONGOING

The improvement cycle curves back on itself for a reason: Once you get to the "end" you continue back around the cycle, but each time you use it at a higher level and apply it to a more complex problem of student learning. As the practice of using the improvement cycle to change instruction becomes ingrained in the practice of your school, you may find it becomes easier to know what questions to ask, how to examine the data, and how to support teachers and students. You will also be able to go deeper into the work, asking tougher questions, setting higher goals, and involving more people in the process. The first time around it might have been all you could do to get your faculty to begin thinking about addressing student learning in a proactive way. As you continue, you may find that you need to involve other constituents who have a stake in student learning outcomes, such as families and community members, in the process. By the time you have been doing this kind of work for several years, you might notice that you quite naturally find ways to enlist the support of even more partners in making a difference for student learning.

As you keep the work going, you may also find that you are able to distribute leadership responsibilities more efficiently than you originally could. When your school has developed a solid culture of inquiry, it becomes natural for large numbers of teachers to take active roles in making sure that the school focuses on continuous improvement. Teachers increase their span of interest and responsibility from their own classrooms and grade levels to concern for the school as a whole. The function of your data team may shift as well. Whereas at the beginning only data-team members might have been interested in or capable of analyzing data, as more teachers in your building become comfortable with this work, the skills become more widely spread throughout the faculty. The data team can then graduate to a role of thinking more broadly about what kinds of assessments your school needs in order to determine what it wants to know about student learning, and can even begin conversations with your district about what kinds of central support for this work would be most helpful. With that in mind, the final chapter of this book lays out the most effective ways we have seen districts support schools in using data wisely.

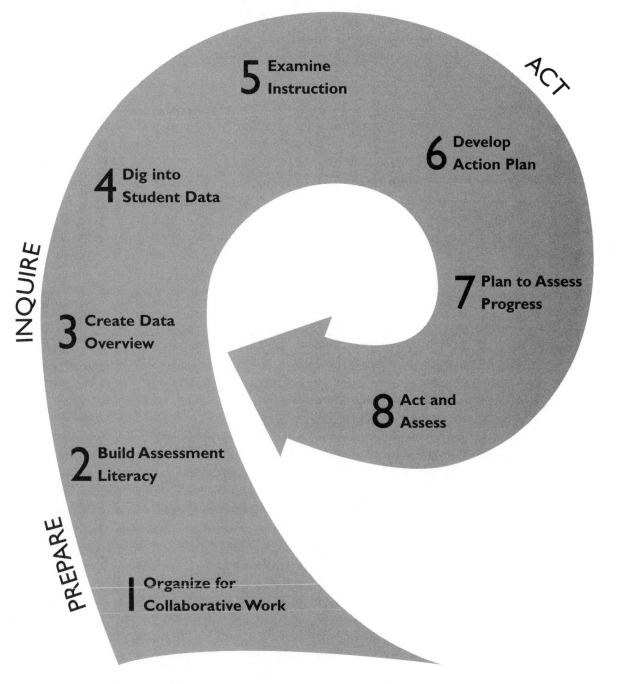

9

ROLES FOR THE DISTRICT CENTRAL OFFICE

Nancy S. Sharkey and Richard J. Murnane

THE PURPOSE OF THIS CHAPTER IS TO PROVIDE SCHOOL superintendents and their leadership teams with an understanding of the roles that district central offices can play, in most districts must play, if schools are to make constructive use of student assessment results. These roles, which we describe below, include providing a data system and software, incentives, skills, and time to do the work. We also argue that it is important for central office teams to model the work.

THE DATA SYSTEM

WHAT SHOULD BE INCLUDED?

An important first step districts can take to support schools' efforts to use student assessment results constructively is to create and maintain a student information system that is accurate and kept up-to-date. Of course, it makes sense for the data system to contain student-specific, detailed results from the state high-stakes assessments—the results schools are under pressure to improve. However, since analysis of these scores always raises more questions than it answers (see chapter 4), the potential to examine multiple data sources is important. For that reason, many districts have found it useful to ask schools to administer benchmark assessments in mathematics and English language arts over the school year and to store results from these tests in the district's central database. Other potentially valuable information to store and make available to schools electronically includes results on midyear and end-of-year course-specific tests. As explained in chapter 4, school data teams often find it valuable to examine not only students' total scores on these examinations, but also skill-specific subscores and responses to individual items. Consequently, it is important that the district data system makes this easy to do.

Given that time spent testing children is time taken from instruction, it is important to verify that test results are useful in diagnosing the strengths and limitations of children's knowledge and the extent to which they have mastered skills included in state learning standards and in the district's curriculum. For example, if the curriculum and state standards emphasize skill at responding to open-ended questions, it makes sense for the assessments to include open-ended questions. If the curriculum and standards focus on multistep questions, the assessment should as well. We have seen many schools analyzing student assessment data only to realize that the district's high-stakes, external assessment did not match the district's curriculum policy. For example, an eighth-grade math test assesses algebra skills not covered in the district's curriculum until ninth grade. If the assessments do not match the curriculum and standards, teachers and administrators are unlikely to believe that the assessment results are accurate measures of what students know and can do. Consequently, they are unlikely to buy into the idea that looking carefully at student assessment results is a valuable use of their scarce time.

As we explained in chapter 3, school-based data teams often want to examine the relative performance of students with different characteristics. For that reason, it makes sense for the districtwide database to contain information about individual students, including gender, race, and ethnicity, special education status, language-minority status, and free or reduced-price lunch eligibility. Some school data teams also want to examine the performance of groups of students that participate in special programs, such as tutoring or after-school programs. Having this information recorded on the district database makes these tasks much easier to accomplish. Since enrollment in programs like tutoring changes rapidly, it is important to implement a strategy for keeping the information up-to-date.

HOW SHOULD THE DATA BE ORGANIZED?

It makes sense to store student data at the individual level so that data teams have the flexibility to examine assessment results for students grouped in a variety of ways. It is also important that the data system track students over time, as they switch schools and complete additional assessments. To do this, each student must have a personal identification number. A growing number of states are assigning identification numbers to students when they first enter a public school in the state. When districts use these same numbers, the tasks of following students from district to district and merging results from state- and district-administered assessments become easier. Updating the district's data system regularly so that records accurately reflect the school each student is attending and the classes each student is taking is critical. School data teams will persevere in making sense of student assessment results only if they find that the information in the district's database is accurate and up-to-date.

Districts with relatively small numbers of students may find it sufficient to store student data in a database management program such as Microsoft Access. However, to provide support for a large number of data teams making multiple varied queries about student data, larger districts are likely to find it necessary to purchase a data warehouse.

WHAT SOFTWARE SHOULD BE USED?

Once all pertinent information is located in a well-supported district data warehouse or database, the district must give schools computer software to analyze the data. This may be as simple as making sure that every school has access to the Internet and to a spreadsheet program such as Microsoft Excel. However, many districts we have worked with provide all schools with customized software that allows data teams to easily create the types of graphs illustrated in chapter 3.

It is important to recognize that the capacity to analyze student assessment data will vary widely across schools. This creates the challenge of providing tools that satisfy the needs of data teams doing quite sophisticated work and those that are just beginning. This is a challenge because, typically, the more sophisticated the analyses a software system will support, the more complex its design will be and the more difficult it will be to use.

We have seen districts deal with the "power versus ease of use" trade-off in a variety of ways. Some provide all schools with basic reports that school staffs will likely start with when creating a basic data overview of the school. These basic reports can be preprogrammed in the district's data system, enabling school staffs to retrieve them easily for their own schools. One district calls these reports the "Top Ten" and distributes paper copies to school administrators as well as making them available online. Once these overviews have been discussed by administrators, the data team, and the school faculty, members of the school data team can engage in the deeper data work that discussion of these reports will prompt. A variant of this strategy used by another district is to create an easy-to-use software system that allows schools to address an important but limited set of questions. Once school data teams have mastered this software and demand more powerful tools, the district provides training in Excel and a means of downloading the school's data into that software tool.

As school data teams become good at the work, they make greater demands of the data. For example, one data team we worked with wanted to know how students who had been in their building for at least two years had fared on the state assessments. Another wanted to investigate whether students who had math for their first-period class did less well on the state math exam than students who had math later in the day. Designing data and software systems that allow data teams to answer such detailed questions efficiently and also engage the novice user after only a little training is a significant design challenge. District staff need to be prepared to support schools at all stages in their learning and to help schools to share novel display strategies and creative and informative analyses.

MAKE OR BUY?

Districts that want to give schools the tools to do the work described in this book need to decide whether to create data and software systems in-house or purchase them from an external vendor. Each alternative has advantages and disadvantages, the importance of which will depend on local circumstances, including in-house technical capabilities. One district that we have worked with created its own Web-based database system, which enabled schools to combine student characteristics and high-stakes assessment data with formative data generated at the school level. An advantage of this choice was that because many central office departments and school representatives were involved in the design and implementation of the data system, many clients were ready to use the product. A disadvantage was that the process was slow. It took more than a year to provide schools the tools for basic analyses like those described in chapter 3, and the development process is ongoing three years later.

Another district we have worked with contracted with a vendor to provide reports and analyses of student assessment data to administrators, teachers, parents, and students. Some vendors provide data warehouse and software systems that will support very sophisticated data analyses. Some also provide formative assessments and teacher professional development tailored to meet needs identified in the assessment results. An advantage of purchasing products and services from external vendors is that they typically are prepared to act quickly. Of course, these products come at a cost, typically ranging from $5 to $75 per student.

WHO HAS ACCESS TO WHAT DATA?

Because student information is confidential, every district with a central data system must have a process for determining who has access to what data for which students. In several districts we work with, teachers could not access the assessment results of their former students. Since results from the state tests administered in May were not available until September, this meant that they could not learn whether students they had taught the previous year were able to demonstrate proficiency on the skills they had emphasized. The importance of remedying this flaw in the access system seems straightforward. However, other access questions are more difficult. For example, should teachers be able to access test scores of the students taught by other teachers in their schools? Should math teachers be able to access reading scores for the students to whom they teach math? These are two examples of the many access questions that arise when school faculties attempt to examine student assessment results.

One district we worked with adopted a decentralized solution to the access issue. The data system was organized so that members of the data team in each school had access to all student assessment information for students currently at the school. Each school's principal determined the composition of the school's data team. In some schools, the principal took on the primary role for data analysis. In other schools, a vice principal or specially designated department head had primary access to data. Teachers who wanted to work on data-related issues for the entire school could volunteer to join the data team.

INCENTIVES

While the work of learning from student assessment results can be a powerful strategy for driving instructional improvement and can also be personally rewarding, it is time-consuming and is not part of the common practice of most schools. Creating incentives for schools to do this work is one of the many challenges district leaders face. We have seen some districts require that the whole-school improvement plan (WSIP) that schools must periodically create be based on analyses of student assessment results. Since schools with compelling WSIPs are given more autonomy and control over resources than schools that lack good plans, there is an incentive to do the analysis work well. For this strategy to contribute to improved student learning, it is important that the central office officials responsible for supervising schools pay attention to WSIPs. School leaders treat the creation of action plans seriously only if deputy superintendents pay attention to whether schools actually carry out the plans described in the WSIPs.

NECESSARY SKILLS

While incentives are important, they are not enough. To use student assessment results constructively, school staffs need a variety of skills, including the ability to 1) understand, interpret, and use assessment data correctly (assessment literacy); 2) use software to access data and create and understand graphic displays of assessment results; 3) participate productively in group conversations and decisions about potentially threatening topics; 4) develop, implement, and assess action plans to improve instruction. The district central office has a major role to play in organizing and supporting the requisite professional development.

ASSESSMENT LITERACY

To interpret score reports from different tests, teachers and administrators need to understand scales, benchmarks, and percentile ranks. To appreciate what inferences are appropriate to make from assessment results, educators also need to understand other concepts explained in chapter 2, such as measurement and sampling errors, validity, and reliability. In our work with schools, we have observed two strategies that appear to help school-based data teams acquire elements of assessment literacy: modeling good practice and providing expertise on an as-needed basis. One district we have worked with created a sample WSIP that modeled the appropriate use of student assessment results. Since every school is required to create a WSIP, the model plan attracted considerable attention. This district also has a research office staffed by people with the skills to answer the many questions that arise as school-based teams work to make sense of test score reports.

USING THE DATA SYSTEM

In chapter 3, we described the types of data displays that school staffs may find useful in catalyzing conversations about student assessment results. We have seen district central offices engage in several activities to help school-based educators learn to use the district's data system and create effective graphic displays. One is professional development specifically directed to teaching these skills. A second is preprogramming software so that school-based users can produce commonly requested graphs for specific groups of students by following a few instructions. Of course, for this to work, it is necessary to have staff available to answer the many questions that arise concerning how to follow even the most carefully written instructions. A third is the creation of an online help system.

GROUP PROCESSES AND COLLABORATION

A theme of this book is that to contribute to instructional improvements, the work of analyzing student assessment results needs to be done collaboratively. Some teachers feel uncomfortable participating in many of the activities described in this book, including brainstorming about potential explanations for patterns in student assessment results and discussing their students' work with other teachers. Some teachers are reluctant to be observed by other teachers because this runs so contrary to the closed-classroom-door culture of their schools. It is worth remembering that many building and district administrators come out of schools with closed-door cultures and have no experience in creating a culture in which teachers work together to do the work described in this book.

We have suggested that using protocols to structure conversations about student performance and instructional strategies can help school faculties to create a "data wise" school culture. In our experience, many school leaders are not aware of the value of protocols and how to use them. We see this as a potentially valuable focus of professional development for school leaders, and we reiterate our belief that the term "data wise" can encompass school-based educators with a variety of job titles.

As we explained in chapter 3, having all teachers and administrators take their students' high-stakes test has been an eye-opening experience in some schools we have worked with, one that catalyzed constructive conversations about teaching and learning. Districts can facilitate this activity by ensuring that school staffs have copies of previously administered tests and answers available.

Collaboratively creating scoring rubrics and then scoring student papers in groups also builds collegiality and teacher knowledge. Teachers report that scoring statewide assessments was a powerful form of professional development. It not only taught them to understand what the assessment was asking, but also increased their understanding of the state curriculum standards and what different levels of student performance actually looked like. This activity can help teachers develop a common language of assessment and instruction. Typically, however, the teachers who are sent to grade statewide tests are the "specialists," or teachers who are already recognized for their skills. Districts might expand the cadre of teachers who participate in such exercises so that more teachers have access to these learning opportunities and can share what they have learned with other teachers at their schools.

DEVELOPING, IMPLEMENTING, AND ASSESSING ACTION PLANS

The recurring theme of this book is that analyzing student assessment results is a critical part of effective instructional improvement strategies. Chapter 5, for example, presented ways school staffs can identify *current* teaching practices at the school, and chapter 6 discussed how teachers and administrators can create instructional action plans that move teachers from analyzing data to developing strategies for improvement. In our experience, however, we have found that many school faculties need help in moving from an understanding of a student learning problem to the design and implementation of an effective instructional improvement plan.

Districts can support the work proposed in both chapters by providing professional development in content and pedagogy. In some districts we have worked with, professional development is provided through coaches (also known as specialists), who receive professional development from the district's central office and then share what they have learned at the schools where they work. These coaches typically spend part of their time working with large groups of teachers (for example, leading a session on exploring assessment results). They also spend part of their time in classrooms, modeling, assisting with, and observing lessons. An important and often missing step in using coaches to support instructional improvement is teaching them the skills described in this book. Unless coaches understand how to do the steps of the improvement cycle, they will not be able to help schools carry them out.

Employing coaches is not the only way to increase teachers' instructional capacity. In most schools, there are teachers with the expertise to help other teachers develop greater pedagogical and content knowledge. By creating opportunities for teachers to learn from each other (for example, by visiting one another's classrooms and having structured and safe conversations about teaching and learning), districts can take advantage of the expertise that already exists within schools and the district while increasing capacity still further.

TIME

The school day in most districts does not afford teachers and administrators enough time to work together to systematically examine student assessment results and to translate their acquired knowledge into instructional improvements. One district we worked with negotiated a contract with its teachers union that called for slightly longer school days four days per week and an early release day for students once each week. Teachers meet for professional development after students leave on the early release day. Half of this time each month is dedicated to district-selected professional development topics, and half is set aside for topics selected by school-based decisionmaking teams. Teachers reported that they had used some of their time creating rubrics together and scoring student work based on the rubrics. Professional development time also was allocated to look at external assessment results and to plan instruction accordingly.

Teachers often need time not only to talk with each other, but also to talk with students. As explained in chapter 4, conversations with students can be an important data source for understanding what they know and don't know and, perhaps more importantly, why. Talking with students in this way, however, can be difficult in the typical instructional schedule. If districts value the information gleaned from conversations between students and teachers about student work, they could encourage schools to adopt schedules that build in time for such conversations.

Observing colleagues in the same school teach can provide teachers with practical instructional ideas, can help foster mentoring relationships, and can further discussions about instructional strategies. For these reasons, many schools we have worked with see this activity as central to their strategy for creating consistent, effective instructional programs. Some school districts facilitate this activity by paying for substitutes to cover the classrooms of visiting instructors.

It is quite possible that there might not be enough common planning time, even if the district has created additional shared professional development time. In these cases, the district might compensate teachers if they spend their own time on professional development activities pertaining to data use. For example, one district negotiated a stipend for teachers who participated in a set number of hours of professional development activities that exceeded the number of hours required by contract. This extra pay provided teachers with the incentive to explore ways to improve their instructional practices, even when the district could not provide additional time in the school day for this endeavor.

MODELING THE WORK

One way a school district's leaders can support schools' efforts to learn from student assessment results is to model the process. They could create a data team to analyze the results of the district's students on the state assessments. The data team could then examine other sources of evidence on student achievement to make sense of patterns in the state assessment results and to identify a student learning problem. The district data team could then examine its existing instructional initiatives with the goal of identifying a problem of practice. An expanded team could then create an action plan, put it into practice, and assess the extent to which it affected classroom instruction and student achievement. This would be new work for most members of the central office data team, and many would be hard pressed to develop the skills and find the time. However, these are the same challenges schools face. A central office leadership team that embraces this work sends a strong message to the district's schools about its importance.

Finally, the district can signal the importance of the process of learning from assessment results by sticking with it. This includes celebrating the successes, setting new goals, and returning to the improvement cycle. District central offices that want schools to become data wise need to become data wise themselves.

SELECTED PROTOCOLS

THROUGHOUT THIS BOOK, we have described a number of strategies that school leaders can use to increase the effectiveness of collaborative efforts to use data to improve instruction. Many of the strategies we have offered involve using protocols to structure conversations about data.

In most cases, we described protocols in the chapters where they are relevant and used chapter end notes to direct readers to websites where they can obtain more complete information. Here we provide instructions for three protocols that we have found to be particularly helpful in involving groups of educators in meaningful data work.

PROTOCOL 1: CONSTRUCTING THE IMPROVEMENT PROCESS

Purpose

* To help a group of people come to a common understanding of how they view the improvement process.

* To allow people to discover for themselves that the improvement process is not linear and that there is no one "right" way to do it.

Notes

* This exercise takes about 45 minutes to complete; feel free to adapt suggested times as needed.

* Break group into teams of three to five people each. (This is a hands-on activity; it is important that groups be small so that everyone can actively participate.)

* Give each group poster paper, tape, markers, and an envelope containing eight squares of paper, each containing one step of the improvement cycle described in this book. Also include a couple of blank squares of paper for participants to add their own steps during the exercise.

Steps

1. 15 min: Ask groups to use the supplies given to create a visual representation of how schools engage in the improvement process. Tell them they can feel free to add, change, duplicate, or delete any of the steps included in the envelope.

2. 5 min: Ask groups to discuss where their school is in the process they have just described.

3. 10 min: Have groups post their creations around the room, and ask people to do a "gallery walk" to see each other's work.

4. 10 min: Ask people what they noticed in doing the exercise, and what they noticed in doing the walk. Ask what steps were missing or unnecessary. Key points to bring out are the variety of the processes created and their nonlinear and recursive nature.

5. 5-15 min: (optional, depending on circumstances) Come to an agreement about the improvement cycle that the group will use in their work together, acknowledging that any way of modeling the improvement process is artificial but that to make progress, a group needs to agree on how they will approach the work.

PROTOCOL 2: THE QUESTION FORMULATION TECHNIQUE

(Copyright: The Right Question Project, www.rightquestion.org; used with permission)

Purpose

* To help a group of people fully explore an important issue before jumping in to a discussion of what they are going to do about it.

* To provide a forum in which all voices can be heard, thus increasing the number of ideas generated and leveling the power dynamic.

Notes

* This protocol takes about 45 minutes to complete; adapt suggested times as needed.

* Break group into teams of five to eight people each.

* Pass out a chart pad, tape, and two markers to each group.

* During protocol, circulate around the room and remind people to follow the "two rules" (see Step 2 below).

Steps

1. 2 min: Identify issue. Write the issue you would like the groups to address on chart paper at the front of the room. Issues can be phrased as questions or statements and can be quite general, such as "Using data to improve instruction," or more specific, such as "Why don't more of our tenth graders score in the top proficiency levels of our state exam?"

2. 5-10 min: Brainstorm. Ask groups to brainstorm questions about this issue and to write these questions on their chart paper. Tell people that they have to follow two rules:

   No. 1: Phrase all responses as questions, not statements.

   No. 2: Write questions exactly as stated—no editing questions.

3. 3 min: Examine. Ask groups to look at their brainstormed list, classifying questions as close-ended and open-ended. Allow groups to change the form of any questions if they would like.

4. 5 min: Prioritize. Ask groups to choose the three questions that they think are most important, and then choose the most important of these prioritized questions.

5. 5-8 min: Branch off. Ask groups to write the most important question at the top of a new piece of paper and then brainstorm new questions about it, again following the two rules described above.

6. 3-5 min: Prioritize again. Ask groups to choose the three most important questions.

7. 5 min: Share. Go around the room and ask each group to state their prioritized questions.

8. 10 min: Debrief. Ask people what they noticed in doing this exercise. Key points that may come up include the way this process keeps a group from jumping to solutions, allows many voices to be heard, and allows for deep consideration of an issue.

PROTOCOL 3: THE AFFINITY PROTOCOL[1]

Purpose

* To help a group of people explore the causes of a problem that they have identified.

* To allow all individuals to participate anonymously in generating hypothesized causes.

Notes

* This protocol takes about 45 minutes to complete; adapt suggested times as needed.

* Break group into teams of four to seven people each.

* Pass out chart paper, small adhesive notes (at least 5 per person), and markers to each team.

* This protocol works best if the group has decided what problem they want to dig into before starting the exercise.

Steps

1. 1 min: Ask teams to write the problem to be explored at the top of a piece of chart paper.

2. 5-10 min: Ask individuals to work independently to brainstorm hunches and hypotheses about what might be the causes of the problem. Individuals write each of their ideas on separate adhesive notes.

3. 10 min: Ask individuals to place their adhesive notes randomly on their chart paper. Tell the teams to make a section on the chart paper for items over which they have no control. Then tell the teams to sort the remaining items into classifications, using minimal discussion. It is okay for some notes to stand alone. If there is an idea that goes under more than one grouping, participants can duplicate the idea on a separate adhesive note and include it in two categories. If the item is something over which they have no control, move it to that section of the chart paper.

4. 5 min: Tell teams to create a header for each category and write it on the chart paper. Large categories can be divided into subcategories with subheadings.

5. 5-10 min: Ask teams to choose their top three (or one or two, depending on your purpose for this exercise) causes for the problem, remembering that the best causes to choose are:

    * Things they have control over

    * Things they believe that, if fixed, would have the biggest impact in fixing the problem

6. 5-10 min: If you have more than one team, all teams share their top causes. Ask for a few comments about what people notice. Ask about whether there is any pattern in where these choices came from.

FURTHER READING

FOR READERS WHO WOULD LIKE additional support in their efforts to use student data to improve learning and teaching, we have compiled the following suggestions for further reading. The first section, "General," includes resources that are helpful for all phases of improvement. The other three sections align with the sections of this book and the book's improvement process: Prepare (chapters 1 and 2), Inquire (chapters 3, 4, 5), and Act (chapters 6, 7, 8). Within each section, sources are offered by topic. While this inventory of resources is by no means comprehensive, it includes those we have found helpful in our own work of using data to improve learning and teaching.

GENERAL

Several resources complement our book in describing how to use data in schools. In particular, Victoria L. Bernhardt's *Data Analysis for Continuous School Improvement* (Larchmont, NY: Eye on Education, 2004, 2nd ed.) and Ruth S. Johnson's *Using Data to Close the Achievement Gap: How to Measure Equity in Our Schools* (Thousand Oaks, CA: Corwin Press, 2002) offer many helpful tools, templates, and examples from schools. Johnson's work also specifically addresses the issue of using data to understand and solve the problem of disparate levels of achievement among different groups of students. Bernhardt has many other books about using data, most recently a series of books specific to high schools, middle schools, and elementary schools (also available from Eye on Education).

North Central Regional Educational Laboratory (NCREL) has a very useful website with tools, resources, and a detailed "data primer" that walks you through the process of using data (see http://www.ncrel.org/datause/). A brief video of two schools that use data is also available from NCREL (see http://www.ncrel.org/datause/tools/explore.php).

Finally, *The Power of Protocols: An Educator's Guide to Better Practice* by Joseph P. McDonald, Nancy Mohr, Alan Dichter, and Elizabeth C. McDonald (New York: Teachers College Press, 2003) is a rich resource of guidelines for a variety of conversations among educators. While the book is not specifically about "using data," we have found it valuable in our work because using data is fundamentally about helping people have conversations about what the data means and what to do about it.

PREPARE

GETTING STARTED

Short readings can be useful for sharing with a faculty or data team to start a conversation about why and how to use data. Here we offer several possibilities. Mike Schmoker, in "First Things First: Demystifying Data Analysis" (*Educational Leadership* 60, no. 5, 2003, pp. 22-24; http://pdonline.ascd.org/pd_online/contemp_s_lead/el200302_schmoker. html), argues that schools should focus their school improvement efforts on simple questions of student performance that can be answered using data. Douglas B. Reeves describes several schools' strategies for making data visible to share expertise and celebrate successes in *Accountability for Learning: How Teachers and School Leaders Can Take Charge* (Alexandria, VA: Association for Supervision and Curriculum Development, 2004, pp. 28-45). And in "Uses and Abuses of Data" (http://enc.org/features/focus/archive/data/document.shtm?input=FOC-003004-index), Nancy Love emphasizes that data can be abused, but that using it the "right way" while not focusing on increasing test scores will result in raised test scores anyway. Finally, in "The Work of Leadership" (*Harvard Business Review,* January-February 1997, pp. 124-134), Ronald A. Heifetz and Donald L. Laurie describe the work of leading change as including both "technical" and "adaptive" challenges, and provide strategies for leading adaptive change. This article is not education specific, but it succinctly addresses challenges that are highly relevant to the work of using data in schools.

For further discussion of the role of using data with a particular emphasis on the role of technology, see *Information Technology for Schools: Creating Practical Knowledge to Improve Student Performance,* edited by Bena Kallick and James M. Wilson (San Francisco: Jossey-Bass, 2001). The book approaches data-based decisionmaking from the perspective of "knowledge creation," and emphasizes the collection of school-based data as a way to form a practitioner knowledge base of what works in the classroom.

The current context for using data to improve teaching and learning includes the No Child Left Behind Act (NCLB) of 2001, which is the reauthorization of the Elementary and Secondary Education Act. Educators who want to know more about what NCLB actually says will find the U.S. Department of Education website helpful. The full text of NCLB is available there, along with additional information (see http://www.ed.gov/policy/elsec/leg/esea02/index.html). In a short essay, Kati Haycock and Ross Weiner of The Education Trust aim to explode common misperceptions about adequate yearly progress (AYP) under NCLB ("Adequate Yearly Progress Under NCLB," paper presented at the Implementing the No Child Left Behind Act Conference, Washington, D.C., 2003; available at http://www.ppionline.org/documents/Ed_NCLB_0403.pdf, pp. 27-31).

ASSESSMENT

CRESST (National Center for Research on Evaluation, Standards, and Student Testing) offers a glossary and quick overview of useful assessment terms that can be shared with faculty (see http://cresst96.cse.ucla.edu/CRESST/pages/glossary.htm). Leslie Walker Wilson's *What Every Teacher Needs to Know about Assessment* (Larchmont, NY: Eye on Education, 2005) provides a teacher-oriented description of assessment fundamentals, including a section on "essential measurement concepts." Wilson talks about "assessment" in terms of both standardized tests and classroom assessments. W. James Popham's *Classroom Assessment: What Teachers Need to Know* (Boston: Allyn & Bacon, 2002, 3rd ed.) describes a variety of assessments and is more like a textbook on assessments for teachers.

INQUIRE

DATA DISPLAYS

The classic source for guidance on high-quality data displays is Edward R. Tufte's work; see, e.g., *The Visual Display of Quantitative Information* (Cheshire, CT: Graphics Press, 1983). For a more education-focused, concise description, see Edie L. Holcomb's *Getting Excited about Data: Combining People, Passion, and Proof to Maximize Student Achievement* (Thousand Oaks, CA: Corwin Press, 2004, 2nd ed.), which offers several ideas about using data, including how to create data displays.

LEARNING AND TEACHING

Part of the inquiry process is building a shared understanding of effective learning and teaching. We have found two resources, both of which are grounded in research, particularly helpful for building this understanding. The first is the second edition of *Dimensions of Learning: Teacher's Manual* by Robert J. Marzano et al. (Alexandria, VA: Association for Supervision and Curriculum Development, 1997). The authors describe five "dimensions of learning": attitudes and perceptions, acquiring and integrating knowledge, extending and refining knowledge, using knowledge meaningfully, and habits of mind. The *Teacher's Manual* also includes many strategies for teaching that support learning in all the dimensions. Many other resources, including videos, are available through the Association for Supervision and Curriculum Development (ASCD) as support for the *Dimensions of Learning* framework (see www.ascd.org).

The second resource is a revision of the original Bloom's taxonomy, *A Taxonomy for Learning, Teaching, and Assessing: A Revision of Bloom's Taxonomy of Educational Objectives* (abridged edition edited by Lorin W. Anderson and David R. Krathwohl; New York: Addison Wesley Longman, 2001). The revision describes educational objectives in terms of two dimensions: knowledge and cognitive processes. The two-dimensional framework is particularly helpful for mapping objectives and thinking about both the "what" and "how" of learning goals, and how they inform teaching and assessing.

Other resources offer insight into the work of improving learning and teaching. Richard F. Elmore, whose work we draw on, particularly in chapter 5, links policy and improvement in a series of essays in *School Reform from the Inside Out: Policy, Practice, and Performance* (Cambridge, MA: Harvard Education Press, 2004). These essays are helpful for school leaders in thinking about internal accountability, professional development, and school improvement; they are also good to share with instructional leadership teams, data teams, and faculty to stimulate discussion. In "Inquiry-Minded Schools: Opening Doors for Accountability," Sharon F. Rallis and Margaret M. MacMullen describe how several schools have created internal accountability through a focus on inquiry, and how external and internal accountability can work together (*Phi Delta Kappan* 81, no. 10, 2000, pp. 766-773; http://www.pdkintl.org/kappan/kral0006.htm).

LOOKING AT STUDENT AND TEACHER WORK

For further information on how to engage in the inquiry process, we recommend several resources. The website www.lasw.org offers numerous resources for looking at student work, including protocols. The website for the National School Reform Faculty (http://www.nsrfharmony.org/default.html) offers resources for collaborative examination of teacher and student work, including protocols, videos, and training for facilitators. The site also includes information on Critical Friends Groups (CFGs), a formal framework for inquiry. Other helpful resources include two books from Project Zero at the Harvard Graduate School of Education, *Making Learning Visible* and *Making Teaching Visible* (published by Project Zero and Reggio Children's Publications); *Looking Together at Student Work* by Tina Blythe, David Allen, and Barbara S. Powell (New York: Teachers College Press, 1999), and *Collaborative Analysis of Student Work: Improving Teaching and Learning* by Georgea M. Langer, Amy B. Colton, and Loretta S. Goff (Alexandria, VA: Association for Supervision and Curriculum Development, 2003).

The website for The Education Trust (see http://www2.edtrust.org/EdTrust/ SIP+Professional+Development/Standards+in+practice.htm) describes an inquiry and professional development process called Standards in Practice (SIP), which helps educators examine student and teacher work in the context of what they want students to know and do. Another approach to inquiry and professional development, teacher action research, is described at George Mason University's Graduate School of Education website (see http://gse.gmu.edu/research/tr/TRaction.shtml). This site offers a comprehensive explanation of teacher action research, a step-by-step explanation of how to conduct an action research project, and a bibliography of action research publications. Finally, *At the Heart of Teaching: A Guide to Reflective Practice* by Grace Hall McEntee et al. (New York: Teachers College Press, 2003) provides tools, including protocols, for engaging in reflection about teaching and learning.

HYPOTHESES

Two resources that offer a variety of tools for formulating hypotheses about a problem are *Root Cause Analysis: Simplified Tools and Techniques* by Bjørn Andersen and Tom Fagerhaug (Milwaukee, WI: ASQ Quality Press, 2000) and *Rapid Problem-Solving with Post-it®️ Notes* by David Straker (Cambridge, MA: DaCapo Press, 1997). Though neither resource is education specific, both are easily applied to an educational context.

VIDEOS

Finding good videos of teaching is always a challenge. While the best resources are often within your own building, sometimes it can be helpful to watch videos of teachers outside your own school. We have drawn on the following resources. The TIMSS (Trends in International Math and Science Study) videos are wonderful for showing math lessons from various countries. Information about the videos, including ordering information, is available at http://nces.ed.gov/timss/Video.asp. A detailed website that includes video footage of a complete secondary literacy lesson can be found at http://www.goingpublicwithteaching.org/yhutchinson/. The Boston Plan for Excellence has made several videos of teaching in Boston, which you can order at http://www.bpe.org/whatsnew.aspx#Video. Finally, the Association for Supervision and Curriculum Development (ASCD) has videos available for a variety of topics at www.ascd.org.

ACT

USING DATA

The February 2003 edition of *Educational Leadership*, which can be ordered from ASCD (www.ascd.org), includes several good articles about using data that can be shared with faculty. Two articles that offer particular insights to inform action are "A Tale of Two Schools' Data" by Beverly Parsons (pp. 66-68) and "The Seductive Allure of Data" by W. James Popham (pp. 48-51). Parsons compares two schools' use of data—one just looks for improved test scores, the other collects implementation data to provide a better understanding of how improvement efforts are proceeding. Popham argues that only data that can inform instruction is worth collecting and sets out characteristics of instructionally useful data, with a particular focus on teacher-created assessments.

PROFESSIONAL DEVELOPMENT

The resources on high-quality professional development are too numerous to mention in this book. Here we do offer a few resources that provide different perspectives on collaborative professional development. First, the Boston Plan for Excellence has a wealth of information on Collaborative Coaching and Learning (CCL), a model for ongoing professional development and inquiry developed in the Boston Public Schools. "Getting Started in CCL" provides an overview of the model and advice from Boston principals, teachers, and coaches (available online at http://www.bpe.org/pubs/CCL/Getting%20 Started%20CCL.pdf). In *Creating Professional Learning Communities: A Step-by-Step Guide to Improving Student Achievement through Teacher Collaboration,* edited by Jennifer Cunningham (Dorchester, MA: Project For School Innovation, 2004, vol. 12; www.psinnovation.org), teachers at the Richard J. Murphy School in Boston describe how collaboration is built into their daily work. Finally, Eleanor Drago-Severson's *Helping Teachers Learn: Principal Leadership for Adult Growth and Development* (Thousand Oaks, CA: Corwin Press, 2004) is a rich resource for principals in supporting the adults in their building as learners.

ASSESSMENTS

The variety of possible assessments is also beyond the scope of this book to describe. Here we offer a few resources to get you started in thinking about assessments at the school and classroom level. A report from Mid-Continent Research for Education and Learning (McREL) describes strategies for gathering evidence of student learning in the classroom, including different types of items on classroom assessments and student self-assessment ("Gathering Evidence of Learning," 2002, ch. 4, pp. 27-37; http://www.mcrel.org/PDF/Noteworthy/5022IR_NW_Focus.pdf). The Northwest Regional Educational Laboratory (NWREL) website provides sample rubrics and scoring guides that use the 6+1 Trait® Writing model of teaching and assessing writing (see http://www.nwrel.org/assessment/scoring.php). Other examples of rubrics and assessment resources for teachers can be found at Kathy Schrock's guide for educators (see http://school.discovery.com/schrockguide/assess.html). Eye on Education has a number of books about assessment, including several that include performance tasks and rubrics by content area and grade level (see http://www.eyeoneducation.com/index.html). Robert J. Marzano's *Transforming Classroom Grading* (Alexandria, VA: Association for Supervision and Curriculum Development, 2000) discusses how to rethink classroom grading to include a variety of assessments and provide richer information about student understanding. Finally, Grant Wiggins's and Jay McTighe's *Understanding by Design* (Alexandria, VA: Association for Supervision and Curriculum Development, 1998) describes the approach of "backward design," or planning with the end in mind, and includes several practical tools for incorporating assessment into plans for curriculum and instruction (see http://www.ubdexchange.org for more information).

END NOTES

Chapter 1

1. For further guidance about using norm-setting protocols, see http://www. turning-pts.org/tools.htm, and J. P. McDonald, N. Mohr, A. Dichter, and E. D. McDonald, *The Power of Protocols: An Educator's Guide to Better Practice* (New York: Teachers College Press, 2003): pp. 26-28.

2. For a complete description of this protocol, see http://www. turningpts.org/tools/htm.

3. See J. Cunningham, ed., *Creating Professional Learning Communities: A Step by Step Guide to Improving Student Achievement through Teacher Collaboration* (Dorchester, MA: Project for School Innovation, 2004): vol. 12, pp. 34-37.

Chapter 2

1. Massachusetts Department of Education, *Guide to Interpreting the Spring 2001 Reports for Schools and Districts* (Malden, MA: Author, 2001): p. 7.

2. H. D. Hoover et al., *Iowa Tests of Basic Skills Interpretive Guide for School Administrators* (Chicago: Riverside, 1994): p. 14.

3. J. D. Braswell, A. D. Lutkus, W. S. Grigg, S. L. Santapau, B. Tay-Lim, and M. Johnson, *The Nation's Report Card: Mathematics 2000* (NCES 2001-517) (Washington, DC: U.S. Department of Education, National Center for Education Statistics, 2001): p. 54.

4. A. Biemiller, "Teaching Vocabulary: Early, Direct, and Sequential," *American Educator* 25, no. 1 (2001).

5. Massachusetts Department of Education, *Guide to the 2000 MCAS Parent/Guardian Report* (Malden, MA: Author, 2000): p. 5.

6. Braswell et al., *The Nation's Report Card: Mathematics 2000.*

7. D. F. McCaffrey, J. R. Lockwood, D. M. Koretz, and L. S. Hamilton, *Evaluating Value-Added Models for Teacher Accountability* (MG-158-EDU) (Santa Monica, CA: RAND, 2003).

8. D. Koretz, "Preparing Students for the MSPAP Assessments," in Assessment-Based Educational Reform: A Look at Two State Programs, part 2, symposium presented at the annual meeting of the American Educational Research Association, J. Pollack, chair, New York, April 1996.

9. For example, D. Koretz, S. Barron, K. Mitchell, and B. Stecher, *The Perceived Effects of the Kentucky Instructional Results Information System* (KIRIS) (MR-792-PCT/FF) (Santa Monica, CA: RAND, 1996); L. A. Shepard and K. C. Dougherty, "Effects of High-Stakes Testing on Instruction," paper presented at the annual meeting of the American Educational Research Association and National Council on Measurement in

Education, Chicago, April 1996.

10. B. M. Stecher, S. L. Barron, T. Chun, and K. Ross, *The Effects of the Washington State Education Reform on Schools and Classrooms* (CSE Tech. Rep. No. 525) (Los Angeles: University of California, National Center for Research on Evaluation, Standards, and Student Testing, 2000).

11. Adapted from D. Koretz, R. L. Linn, S. B. Dunbar, and L. A Shepard, "The Effects of High-Stakes Testing: Preliminary Evidence About Generalization Across Tests," in The Effects of High-Stakes Testing, symposium presented at the annual meetings of the American Educational Research Association and the National Council on Measurement in Education, R. L. Linn, chair, Chicago, April 1991, and reprinted here with permission of the first author.

12. For example, B. Jacob, *Accountability, Incentives and Behavior: The Impact of High-Stakes Testing in the Chicago Public Schools* (Working Paper W8968) (Cambridge, MA: National Bureau of Economic Research, 2002); S. P. Klein, L. S. Hamilton, D. F. McCaffrey, and B. M. Stecher, *What Do Test Scores in Texas Tell Us?* (Issue Paper IP-202) (Santa Monica, CA: RAND, 2000), accessed January 12, 2004, from http://www.rand.org/publications/IP/IP202/); D. Koretz and S. I. Barron, *The Validity of Gains on the Kentucky Instructional Results Information System (KIRIS)* (MR-1014-EDU) (Santa Monica, CA: RAND, 1998).

Chapter 3

1. We learned the Continuum Protocol from a member of the National School Reform Faculty. For more information on the National School Reform Faculty, see www.nsrfharmony.org.

Chapter 4

1. There are many useful protocols for looking at student work, including the Collaborative Assessment Conference, Consultancy, and Standards in Practice. For more information, see http://www.lasw.org/methods/html and http://www2.edtrust.org/EdTrust/SIP+Professional+Development/.

2. For a description of this protocol, see http://www.lasw.org/Slice_descript.html and *Power of Protocols*, pp. 84-91.

Chapter 5

1. The authors are indebted to Richard Elmore for many conversations about problems of practice and what it means to examine and improve instruction.

2. This "why-why-why" diagram is from the Thomas A. Edison Middle School in Boston, Massachusetts. The authors are very grateful to the Edison School for permission to include an example of their improvement work in this chapter.

3. The authors learned this concept of the instructional core from Richard Elmore. For further elaboration of the idea, see Elmore's essay "Getting to Scale with Good Educational Practice" in his book *School Reform from the Inside Out: Policy, Practice, and Performance* (Cambridge, MA: Harvard Education Press, 2004).

4. For a good description of the Think Aloud process, see *Reading for Understanding: A Guide to Improving Reading in Middle and High School Classrooms* by Ruth Schoenbach, Cynthia Greenleaf, Christine Cziko, and Lori Hurwitz (San Francisco: Jossey-Bass, 1999).

Chapter 6

1. The authors would like to thank and credit Harvard professor Richard Elmore for clarifying the connection between the problem of practice and the school's overall strategy for improvement.

2. For a complete description of how to set up World Café Conversations, see http://www.theworldcafe.com/twcrg.html.

3. G. Polya, *How to Solve It: A New Aspect of Mathematical Method* (Princeton, NJ: Princeton University Press, 2004).

4. For an excellent description of the value of articulating these kinds of theories, see C. Weiss, *Evaluation: Methods for Studying Programs and Policies*, 2nd ed. (Upper Saddle River, NJ: Prentice-Hall, 1998): ch. 3.

5. This description of professional development draws on work by Elizabeth A. City and Sara Schwartz in which they reviewed research on the characteristics of professional development that makes a difference in student achievement. E. A. City and S. Schwartz, *Rigorous, Relevant Research.* Unpublished manuscript, 2004.

Chapter 7

1. For an example of this kind of technology, see the Classroom Performance System described at eInstruction.com.

2. Other commercially available diagnostic reading assessments we have seen schools use include: the Qualitative Reading Inventory (QRI), the Developmental Reading Assessment (DRA) for grades K-3, the Analytic Reading Inventory (ARI) for grades 4-8, and the Informal Reading Inventory (IRI) for grades 9-12. Other assessments may generate medium-term data that are less useful for diagnostic purposes but are better adapted to measuring progress over time. One such instrument is the Scholastic Reading Inventory (SRI), which provides a measure of reading comprehension that can be compared to grade level targets that increase progressively each year from grades 1-12. One advantage to the SRI is that the difficulty level of children's literature can be measured using the same scale as SRI reading comprehension scores. This means that teachers, students, and parents can find texts at the

student's comfort level in addition to measuring progress as the student becomes able to read increasingly difficult texts. In some districts, the SRI is administered in the fall, winter, and spring. Results are used in conjunction with teacher input and other achievement data to screen students for special programs, including summer school.

Chapter 8

1. For a complete description, see http://www.instituteforlearning.org/lw.html.

2. For practical tips for getting this type of observation going in schools, see chapter 3 in J. Cunningham, ed., *Creating Professional Learning Communities: A Step by Step Guide to Improving Student Achievement through Teacher Collaboration,* vol.12 (Dorchester, MA: Project For School Innovation, 2004). Available through www.psinnovation.com.

3. For complete information about the Success Analysis Protocol, see http://www.smallschoolproject.org/PDFS/success.pdf; http://www.nsrfnewyork.org/articles/SuccessAnalysisProtocol.doc; http://www.smp.gseis.ucla.edu/downloads/success_analysis_protocol.pdf; and *Power of Protocols* (New York: Teachers College Press, 2003): pp. 60-62.

Selected Protocols

1. Other versions of this protocol can be found in V. L. Bernhardt, *Data Analysis for Continuous School Improvement,* 2nd ed. (Larchmont, NY: Eye on Education, 2004): pp. 150-152, and B. Andersen and T. Fagerhaug, *Root Cause Analysis: Simplified Tools and Techniques* (Milwaukee, WI: ASQ Quality Press, 2000): pp. 99-102.

ABOUT THE CONTRIBUTORS

Kathryn Parker Boudett is a faculty member at the Harvard Graduate School of Education (HGSE), where she teaches a course for Boston Public School educators and graduate students about using data to improve instruction, and also conducts research about how to best structure professional development on this topic.

Tom Buffett, a scholar of organizational development and recent HGSE graduate, taught sixth grade before joining the national faculty of the UCLA School Management Program. He consults with states, districts, and individual schools on developing and using information systems to improve policy and practice. He teaches courses on school leadership and action research.

Jonna Sullivan Casey is director of the Richard J. Murphy School's extensive array of out-of-school-time programs—PRIME TIME After-School Program, Summer STARS, and Saturday Scholars. She was a second-grade teacher and, prior to working in the Boston Public Schools, was purchasing director for Sodexho, USA.

*Elizabeth A. City has taught in North Carolina, Massachusetts, and Russia. She has also been a principal in Durham, North Carolina, and a school coach in Boston. She teaches a course in using data to aspiring principals in Boston's School Leadership Institute.

*Sarah E. Fiarman taught grades 3-6 in Massachusetts and is a National Board Certified Teacher. She leads workshops for teachers in how to build learning communities, use portfolios, and implement antibias curricula, and teaches student teachers in the Boston Public Schools how to use data to improve their teaching.

*Shannon T. Hodge, a National Certified Counselor, has worked as a high school counselor, guidance director, and school testing coordinator in Indiana. She consults with principals and teachers in the Boston Public Schools on understanding data and using assessments to drive and inform school improvement.

*Melissa Kagle is a researcher and curriculum writer for Math in a Cultural Context, a project of the University of Alaska Fairbanks aimed at improving the school achievement of Alaska Native students through a math curriculum based on the knowledge of Yup'ik Eskimo elders. She has taught math and science in public schools in Alaska, California, and Vermont.

Jane E. King is principal of the McCormack Middle School in Boston. A career-change educator, she is a former Boston Public School parent and activist.

Daniel M. Koretz is a professor of education at HGSE, where he teaches courses in educational measurement. He began his career as a special education teacher in Parkrose, Oregon. He was formerly a policy analyst with the Congressional Budget Office and a researcher with RAND.

Gerardo Martinez has been principal for four years at the Mary E. Curley Middle School in Jamaica Plain, Massachusetts. He taught English language arts for six years at the Taft Middle School in Boston, with the last two years focused on literacy development strategies for teachers. He holds a master's degree in educational administration from the University of Massachusetts Boston.

Ethan Mintz is the codesigner of the Formative Assessment of Student Thinking in Reading (FAST-R), currently being used in the Boston Public Schools. He is coeditor of *The Complex World of Teaching: Perspectives from Theory and Practice* (with J. T. Yun), and consults with several school districts to help schools, teachers, and school leaders understand and analyze data for the purpose of making instructional decisions. He is a faculty member at the Indiana University School of Education.

*Liane Moody worked for the Boston Plan for Excellence, where she helped design and implement MyBPS Assessment, an online assessment data analysis tool for the Boston Public Schools. She teaches a course on data-based decision-making in the Leadership and Education department at the University of Massachusetts Boston.

Richard J. Murnane, an economist, is the Thompson Professor of Education and Society at HGSE. He started his career as a high school math teacher in Houston, Washington, and Baltimore. He has worked with the Boston Public Schools since 2001 to build the capacity of schools to make constructive use of student assessment results.

*Jennifer Price was a teacher and a school administrator in Massachusetts before entering the doctoral program at HGSE. Her current research interests are focused on district and school resource allocation and their relationship to student achievement. She plans to pursue either a principalship or a superintendency upon completion of her degree.

Mary Russo is principal of the Richard J. Murphy School, a 950-student K-8 school in Boston. She has been a principal for 14 years and is a National Distinguished Principal. She has taught at all grade levels—elementary, middle, and high school.

*Nancy S. Sharkey has helped design and teach a course on using data for instructional improvement, and has worked intensively with one Boston high school engaged in that process. Her research explores how and why teachers use student assessment data and the role districts play. She began her career as sixth-grade math and science teacher in Long Beach, California.

*Jennifer L. Steele has worked as an elementary school teacher in Virginia and a high school English teacher in California. She has also managed regional teacher recruitment and training for a national test preparation company and served as a research consultant to the Boston Public Schools.

*Mark B. Teoh has been a history teacher in Houston and Philadelphia. He is interested in teacher quality issues in urban districts, and is currently conducting research with the Boston Public Schools that focuses on teacher recruitment and retention.

John B. Willett, a statistician, is the Charles William Eliot Professor of Education at HGSE. His recent research focuses on innovative ways to use longitudinal data and strategies for measuring individual growth. He started his career as a high school physics teacher in Hong Kong.

*Currently a doctoral student at HGSE.

INDEX